DHONI
TOUCH

THE
DHONI
TOUCH

Unravelling the Enigma That Is Mahendra Singh Dhoni

BHARAT SUNDARESAN

FOREWORD BY
RAVI SHASTRI

EBURY
PRESS

An imprint of Penguin Random House

EBURY PRESS

USA | Canada | UK | Ireland | Australia
New Zealand | India | South Africa | China

Ebury Press is part of the Penguin Random House group of companies
whose addresses can be found at global.penguinrandomhouse.com

Published by Penguin Random House India Pvt. Ltd.
4th Floor, Capital Tower 1, MG Road,
Gurugram 122 002, Haryana, India

| Penguin
Random House
India

First published in Ebury Press by Penguin Random House India 2018

Copyright © Bharat Sundaresan 2018
Foreword copyright © Ravi Shastri 2018

All rights reserved

20 19

ISBN 9780143440062

Typeset in Bembo Std by Manipal Digital Systems, Manipal
Printed at Replika Press Pvt. Ltd, India

www.penguin.co.in

To my wife, Isha, for always letting me keep
my hair longer than hers

Contents

Foreword

It's a real pleasure to write this foreword for Bharat who I am sure will portray the best of the great man in his own casual and laid-back style of writing, which, I am sure, will make this book a fascinating read.

My earliest memories of Mahendra Singh Dhoni are unflattering. It was late 2004. There had been talk of an exciting twenty-four-year-old from Ranchi who had been making waves in domestic cricket with his big-hitting, but there was little evidence of his prowess, especially when he made a quiet entry in his first few international games.

The first three games were against Bangladesh, and I can distinctly remember the cluck-cluck in the commentary box when he was dismissed cheaply in the fourth too, this time against Pakistan, always the acid test for any Indian cricketer. Did he really belong at this level?

There wasn't much scope left for debate when Dhoni smashed 148 in the next game he played. Before the year was through, he had thrashed Sri Lanka for an unbeaten 183. A star was born.

For a decade after that, I met Dhoni intermittently. He was player, then captain of India, and I spent most of my time, mic in hand, in the commentary box. Our paths crossed frequently, but given our different jobs, we did not have much time together.

Nonetheless, I marvelled at his rapid growth, as a player, then as a pillar of the Indian team. His work ethic was excellent, as I gathered from those around the Indian team, but even more impressive was his unflappable temperament.

'Captain Cool' may sound clichéd now, but in many ways it was an apt description, for nothing could frazzle Dhoni. I've seen him remain steadfast and inscrutable like a monk in victory and defeat.

With every passing game, my admiration for him only grew, particularly during my stints as the team director in 2014–16, and then as chief coach from mid-2017. Being in the same dressing room gave me greater insight into the player and the man, and in both aspects, he is top class.

Dhoni is an unorthodox cricketer and an unconventional man. His technique, in front of and behind the stumps, is not easily replicable. My suggestion to youngsters is: don't try it, unless it comes naturally. But this does not mean he doesn't put in the hard yards to succeed. In fact, there are few who train and try harder.

As an individual, he is fascinating. A man of few words, his ability to insulate himself from all the brouhaha that surrounds cricket in India—and this gets more cacophonic when a player is successful—is quite remarkable.

He has a sharp street-smart brain and can cut through the clutter—whether on cricketing matters or otherwise—to reach a decision rapidly. Sometimes, the decision can be astounding, leaving people with dropped jaws.

This happened when Dhoni quit Test cricket in the middle of the series against Australia in 2014–15. I had no inkling—nobody did—that this thought was even churning in his mind. When he announced his retirement, everybody was stupefied.

I'll be dishonest if I say I didn't have my doubts he had done the right thing then (especially as a Test player, he could have carried on). But looking back, I think it was the correct decision. Also, brave and selfless. I can't think of another player who would quit the scene having played ninety Tests. The temptation to reach the milestone of 100 would be impossible for most to resist, not to mention the power of captaincy. But Dhoni didn't want to linger on in a format where he believed he wasn't able to give it his all.

Giving up Test cricket, I believe in hindsight, has helped him extend his career by quite a few years. Watching him in the IPL in 2018, I haven't seen him look sharper, fitter and hungrier, which is a kick in the teeth for those who doubted whether he could last this long.

More pertinent is his value in the dressing room. There are always doubts about how a senior player, and a hugely successful former captain at that, would fit in with all the youngsters and a new captain. This requires mature understanding of player and dressing room dynamics, and Dhoni has gelled superbly, being pillar, adviser, mentor, whatever the situation demands, without imposing his ego.

I won't labour on providing Dhoni's career highlights. These are too many and too well known to bear repetition. All I'll say is that in the fifteen years he's been playing international cricket, Dhoni has compiled a body of work which marks him out as a legend. With a capital L.

In fact, I'd use only capital letters to fortify the point. LEGEND.

Mumbai   Ravi Shastri
June 2018

Introduction

'*Woh dekho wahan Dhoni. Kuch cricket mein dhyaan nahi hai uska, style-baazi karta hai bas.* (Look at Dhoni over there. He's not focused on cricket. He's a show pony.),' says a young man about Indian cricket's latest sensation. His companion pitches in: '*Bike ka shaukeen hai. Bike, gaadi, ghadi, buss.* (He loves bikes. He's just about bikes, cars, watches.)' It's February 2005, and I'm at one end of the long, winding lobby at the Taj President (Vivanta now) in Mumbai, happily eavesdropping on these two cricketers talking about Mahendra Singh Dhoni to a bemused senior player. They're in the city for the 2004–05 edition of the Challenger Trophy. Dhoni, who made his international debut only two months earlier, is part of the India Seniors team led by Sourav Ganguly. I'm there waiting for a friend who's also a guest at the hotel.

Meanwhile, at the other end of the lobby, Dhoni steps out of the lift and is immediately swarmed by a gaggle of reporters—many of whom I would go on to share a press box with. I was in college back then and had no ambitions of becoming a journalist. Decked casually in a T-shirt and shorts, Dhoni wades past them, his rust-coloured mane resting on his shoulders. He doesn't say a word. Instead, he shakes his head twice before sauntering into the café for breakfast. Many of the reporters choose to leave, while some stick around the entrance of the café before they too are politely asked to leave by the hotel authorities.

I stand there amused by the melee. Little did I know then that, in less than five years, this joke would be on me too and that I would end up spending hours in hotel lobbies and a lot of other places waiting for Dhoni and get nothing more than that impish smile from him for my efforts.

The character assassination of Dhoni, by the way, isn't over though. The young men aren't done yet.

'*Aur, bhaiya, baal toh dekho. Cricketer lagta bhi hai kya?* (And, brother, look at his hair. Does he even look like a cricketer?),' says one. This last point resonates with me. There I stand not too far from them, my hair nearly till my waist, and very used to these taunts about us, the follicly blessed. There's something about long-haired guys that most Indians don't trust. Funny that, considering they have grown up listening to fables, mythological tales and religious texts where the protagonists all sport long manes and are extolled for their values. But when someone like me does it, it's considered too outré. And you end up hearing the 'same old clichés' that Bob Seger sings about in 'Turn the Page': 'Is it woman, is it man?'

I would have these Tamil *maami*s (aunts) walking up to my mother and consoling her. 'Despite the hair, Usha, your son is a good boy,' they'd say. Their words would also be accompanied by looks of extreme concern. 'Hippy' was a word that would be thrown around rather frivolously. It was as if they were all trying to say, '*Baal toh dekho, aapka beta lagta bhi hai kya?* (Look at his hair. Does he even look like your son?)' My mother's reaction would generally range from surprise to bewilderment and, after a while, she gave up trying to defend me. She would simply nod in agreement. But perhaps at some level, she too bought into the theory that long hair on a man meant trouble.

And it would have been understandable if it was one of those maamis writing off M.S. Dhoni's cricketing credentials at the Taj lobby based only on the length of his hair. But these were two contemporary cricketers, one of whom had already shared a dressing room with the young wicketkeeper batsman from Ranchi.

Within a year anyway, Dhoni's hairstyle was the only thing India and Pakistan were both agreeing on. The mane was there to stay. Even dictator Pervez Musharraf agreed. He, in fact, ordered Dhoni to not even think about chopping his locks off. By then, Dhoni had also smashed two blitzkrieg centuries, including the highest one day international (ODI) score by any wicketkeeper, established himself among the most destructive batsmen in world cricket and was just a year away from taking over as India's T20 captain and winning the inaugural World T20, and chopping off his hair.

It was not like Dhoni was a stranger to petty comments about his appearance. He had, in fact, heard worse. He was used to being typecast as an outcast from a young age. He was used to being an outsider. He was also more crucially used to being an outlier who proved people wrong at every step of his fascinating journey. The way he's managed to do it forms the focus of this book as we try to break into Indian cricket's most popular enigma who has remained a mystery wrapped in a million-dollar bubble. This is not the story of where he's come from or where he's reached. It's about how he got there. It's not about how the Dhoni legend was born or how it was made, but about how his rational approach to life and cricket helped him scale dizzying heights. A man whose feet remained firmly on the ground despite the countless groundbreaking feats that made him the foremost sports star of his generation.

In India, Sachin Tendulkar stands for perfection. The perfect ten. The man who could do no wrong. The man who was marked for greatness, prepared for greatness, and achieved greatness beyond anyone's imagination. He was a prodigy who grew up to be a prodigy.

Dhoni wasn't any of that. Dhoni did the unexpected and continues to do so. He's the quintessential odd man out. He's as cut off from the system as you can be in the context of Indian cricket. He started his career playing for Bihar, a team that pretty much didn't exist on the Indian cricket map. Or it did just because it had to. However, in less than a decade, he ended up putting Ranchi (now in Jharkhand) on the world cricket map.

There's a reason I have started off with his hair. The way he handled his hair over the years is in many ways the way he's dealt with his career, both on and off the field—with common sense, a lot of practical ingenuity and some unmatched foresight. There's of course been a lot of serendipity that's helped him along the way. But you can't hold that against him.

Dhoni held on to his long hair even after becoming an Indian cricketer; perhaps that was because it fit perfectly with the youth icon image that he was targeting to project in terms of endorsements. And when he knew he'd gone past that budding superstar phase and become a full-fledged megastar after the World T20, he got rid of it.

He embraced the power of social media before any of his peers or even those who came after him. Despite being a man whose life story remained closed to the world, he was the first active cricketer to produce a movie about his life in which he revealed only as much as was required to make it a commercial hit. And a movie that required a lot of cajoling from his management team to get him to see—Dhoni is learnt to have watched it eventually in four sittings.

It was the hair that drew me to him in the first place, and not with any great fondness. In the early noughties, sporting a longish mane not only made you a social outcast, you also drew some unkind comparisons of the Bollywood kind. And considering Dhoni and I started growing our hair the same year, chances are he had to deal with the same.

By the time my hair had reached neck-length, I was 'Sanju Baba' (the actor Sanjay Dutt). It only got worse from there. *Tere Naam* released in early 2003, and my hair, unfortunately, had the exact same length as Salman Khan's in the movie. The natural middle parting didn't help either. So, I would find myself serenaded with the song '*Tumse Milna, Baatein Karna*' and have no option but to offer a wry smile in response. By 2004, the hair had moved on to that 'rock star' or, let's say, 'hippy' phase. Then along came Dhoni.

The first time I heard of him was when the rest of the world did, during his exploits on the India A tour to Nairobi in August 2004. It was a friend who alerted me. Dhoni's emergence also coincided with the heavy-metal phase of my life when I was surrounded by long-haired men. So, it wasn't surprising that the first thing I heard about Dhoni was, '*Uske baal dekhe?* (Have you seen his hair?)' And yes, it was unique.

I had never before seen a batsman with hair flowing down from the back of his helmet like Dhoni's was. Yes, Jason Gillespie sported a mullet and even Kapil Dev had experimented with a ponytail in the twilight of his career. But never before had I seen someone with hair like mine— even if it had that very earthy orange shade and looked intentionally straightened—donning a cricket helmet. It didn't even matter then that he was actually hitting the ball almost as hard as Adam Gilchrist. So, the first thought in my mind was, 'Oh no, now everyone will start calling me Dhoni.' And I was so right about that. It was both obvious that Dhoni was a star in the making—not because I had any prophetic powers but because it was just that obvious—and that I would soon go from being a Salman Khan wannabe to a Dhoni wannabe. A few years later it would get worse when Ishant Sharma came on to the stage. But I'm not comfortable talking about that phase yet.

Things did get better for both Dhoni and me as he became more successful. His hair had become the rage of the country and there were many around India sporting the Dhoni hairdo, while mine had long overgrown that length. The more he succeeded, the more he swayed those around me towards believing that it wasn't so bad, after all, for a man to let his hair down, quite literally—you could still be successful, very successful, and have more than a billion people rooting for you. Even those maamis' attitude started changing and now at similar social gatherings where I was used to being frowned upon, I was often the cynosure. '*Apdiye Dhoni maari irrakaane von pullai*. (Your son looks just like Dhoni.),' they would say in Tamil, and my mother would end up beaming.

However, I grew a fondness for Dhoni only after he decided to chop off the locks. It meant that I was no longer being convinced by every new person I met that my hairstyle was inspired by him.

His reaction to the idea of this book and what it would be about was typical Dhoni. I had stopped him just before he entered the gladiator–pit-like pathway towards the dressing room at the Maharashtra Cricket Association (MCA) stadium and told him, 'I'm writing a book on you. But it's not a biography since you've already released a movie about your life. It'll be my attempt at unravelling your enigma.' The word 'enigma' brought a smile on his face. He never quite committed to either giving me an interview or not giving one for this book. Unfortunately, an interview never happened. Although once before an Indian Premier League

(IPL) training session, he did make a very startling revelation or declaration of Dhoni-esque proportions.

'*Kuch socha?* (Have you given it any thought?),' I asked him. '*Unnees ke baad.* (After the nineteenth.),' he replied. For the record, it was 14 April 2017. I thought that's not bad. There are those who've waited for the proverbial eternity to get Dhoni to talk. I can't obviously be complaining about a five-day wait. And without even trying to mask my delight, I ended up uttering, 'Oh, that means only five days. That's great.' Dhoni immediately spun around and flashing that familiar smile again, said, '*Do hazaar unees ke baad.* (After 2019.)' At first I felt a mixture of despair and anger at being snubbed like this. But in truth, he'd misunderstood my question. It was a period when everyone, probably even the selectors, involved with Indian cricket was either keen on knowing about or gunning for his retirement.

And by the time I could clarify, Dhoni had sauntered off. This was the first of many attempts made during the IPL to get the definitive answer. From that point on, whenever the Rising Pune Supergiant (RPS) had a practice session at their home ground, I was there, stationed at that same spot where I'd informed him about the book. It was right below the dressing rooms and in the path which the players took to enter the ground; with Dhoni you have to always pick the right time and the right place and not just hope to be there. Even those closest to him would agree.

Dhoni would come and Dhoni would leave. He would stop, smile and exchange a few sweet nothings and then move on too swiftly for us to go beyond that. That was our IPL X routine.

Then, during one of these meetings, he went after my hair. '*Tera baal toh usse bhi lamba ho gaya.* (Your hair is longer than hers now.),' he said, pointing at a female standing not too far from me. I retorted asking why he was after my mane. He turned around and said, '*Baal kaatlo, yaar.* (Cut your hair, mate.)'

1

The Hair-raising Tale of Mahi

'*A*rrey, yeh ladki jaisa dikhne wala, dhabhe mein khane wala, cricket kya khelega?* (How can this fellow who looks like a girl, and eats at a dhaba, play cricket?)' That's what the chief selector of the MECON (Metallurgical and Engineering Consultants) Colony team had to say when he first encountered Dhoni and rejected him.

The 'dhabhe mein khane wala' comment had to do with the fact that Dhoni's father was a pump operator at MECON, which meant he was from the 'non-executive' set. The boy's unconventional looks only made it worse.

The D Block that housed the Dhoni family was mainly made up of lower-grade employees, but the advantage was that the MECON stadium was across the road. And the only time the 'executive vs non-executive' divide didn't exist was when Dhoni and his friends indulged in a game of football or cricket at the stadium.

Incidentally, Dhoni's decision to grow his hair had nothing to do with fashion or changing his look. The story goes that Dhoni had never had a *mundan* (getting the head tonsured) as a child. And when he finally did it in 2002, the hair started growing and looking good. He then decided to not cut it for a while and let it grow.

'*Achcha lag raha hai. Rehne do. Anyway, kya farak padta hai.* (It's looking good. Let it be. Anyway, what difference does it make.),' he would tell his friends. To complement their Mahi (it's Mahi and not Maahi when you're in Ranchi) or perhaps because they felt motivated, the rest of the Dhoni gang too began growing their hair, reveals Seemant Lohani, better known as Chittu, his closest friend. However, one by one, they started falling prey to the scissor. The mirror wasn't being kind to them, Chittu insists.

'We all did it. Santosh Lal (who unfortunately passed away a few years ago), Gautam-da and even I tried my hand at it. But only Mahi could pull it off. My face was too small. Not only was his hair looking great, it suited him superbly,' says Chittu.

It wasn't just his detractors in MECON Colony who were bothered by Dhoni's growing mane. Even his school coach, 'Mahi's only coach', according to those in Ranchi, Keshav Banerjee recalls being slightly worried about his favourite pupil. The longish hair, of course, came long after Dhoni had left school and Banerjee would see him in the colony on his motorbike or walking to and back from practice. One day, he couldn't help himself but let his former student know just what he thought of his hair.

'I asked him once about why he wasn't cutting it. He said, "*Dekhte hai na kaisa lagega.* (Let's see how it looks.)," with that same smile. I said, "*Achcha nahi lagta.* (It's not looking good.)" I told him, "You are an adult now. I can't just order you to go cut it." He smiled again and said, "*Baal hi hai, sir. Ek din yeh style bhi change ho jaayega.* (It's only hair, sir. One day this style too will change.),"' says Banerjee. Dhoni was right. The style did keep changing. It, in fact, went through a metamorphosis pretty much every other season. The mane was gone completely soon after Dhoni lifted the first of many titles as captain, the first-ever World T20 crown in 2007. Then, of course, he went for the 'full monty' on the night India won the 50-over World Cup in April 2011, His once rustic, 'wannabe hep', mehndi-coloured long mane might have given way to a more sophisticated crop cut a dozen years later. But during those periods, he never failed to keep up with the times— an undercut spike one day, a quiff the next, not to forget the brash Mohawk he sported during the 2013 IPL; and amazingly, both his local barber in Ranchi and his stylist Sapna Bhavnani have seen their profiles get a boost thanks to their work with his hair.

A year later, in 2008, I was a cricket journalist and covering an international match, an ODI between India and England at the Chinnaswamy stadium in November, and about to come face-to-face with the man himself. It wasn't a meeting that I had thought about or longed for anxiously, to be honest. But as I waited for him to enter the press conference room at the Lalit Hotel on that rainy afternoon, I do remember thinking whether Dhoni would notice the hair. I wanted him to, anyway. I also wanted him to then think about how he'd given up on being *one of us* simply because he couldn't handle it. But nothing happened. My chance at this strange attempt at juvenile one-upmanship had come and gone.

Actually, Dhoni notices everything. He never misses a beat or a note. Those who've known him from the early days in Ranchi swear by this Dhoni characteristic. 'He won't say much. But he observes everything,' you hear every one of them say, almost incessantly. It's something I had always noticed about him at press conferences, and it's a trait that is still there. Most cricketers have their own way of settling down before it starts while the camera crew and reporters sort out their equipment. Dhoni's thing has always been to judiciously arrange all the phones and voice recorders together on the table in front of him so that they're all kind of bunched together. Even now, if he finds a phone, or one with a distinct phone cover, that he has probably not seen before, you'll see him pick it up and check it out.

A few years ago, during a practice session on the eve of an ODI, Dhoni suddenly walked up from behind and said, '*Bahut jyaada badd gaye hai*. (It's become too long.)' That's when I realized that they don't exaggerate when they say Dhoni notices everything. He had noticed the hair, after all. I wouldn't say Dhoni and I are very close. The more tours I did, especially overseas, we did become familiar with each other even if our conversations were mainly random chats on the sidelines of practice sessions.

But this was the first time he'd ever remarked about my hair. However, from that point on, this was the first thing he would talk about every single time we crossed paths. And it was always he who brought it up. It was to become our little in-joke.

Except that one time I asked him about how he'd mustered the courage to actually get rid of his long hair and never grow it to any significant length again almost a decade ago. We were in Harare for India's tour of Zimbabwe in 2016. It was a strange tour for Dhoni where he was captaining a team mainly made up of fringe players, most of whom he'd never shared a dressing room with. He was stuck mostly within the confines of the hotel with this bunch of young guys he was just getting to know. It ended up being a great tour for him even if he didn't score many runs. Dhoni ended up playing mentor and tutor to most of them on and off the field, and by the end of it, he was a refreshed man. It was like he had found a new purpose to continue doing what he was doing. In a career where he'd embraced enough gimmicks to put a World Wrestling Entertainment (WWE) wrestler to shame, he'd just found a new niche.

Then he had a little piece of advice for me. '*Teri biwi kya bolti hai?* (What does your wife say?),' he asked me. 'She doesn't mind it, I guess. She didn't ask me to cut it even for our wedding,' I replied. He then simply smiled at me and in that typical Dhoni fashion, said, 'So do one thing, cut it really short and go surprise her. She'll be happy . . .' and walked away.

Within just six months, he was coaxing me to give it a trim. Incidentally, his insistence on this started the day I told him about the book. I would like to believe it was just a coincidence. It was also the day he was about to meet the press in Pune after he'd announced his resignation as India's ODI and T20 captain. The warehouse-like press conference room next to the massive dog kennel at the MCA stadium resembled a Mumbai local train with barely any standing space. I was near the entrance, right at the back. Dhoni arrived five minutes late. He was welcomed with that unmistakable wispy buzz that accompanies a poignant moment in time. And this was a massive moment. A man, who had held what's considered the most nerve-racking job in world cricket with not much more than some greys to show for it for nearly a decade, was now addressing the media as just another player. Like every one of my colleagues present, I too was revising the question that I had in mind for the man.

It was Dhoni as usual who broke the ice. He did so by targeting my hair again. '*Peeche se samajh nahi raha ki tu hai ya koi ladki khadi hai.* (From behind, I can't make out whether it's you or a girl.),' he said, resulting in giggles around us. Though slightly taken aback, I mumbled back something like, '*Yaar, aap toh yeh mat bolo!* (You of all people shouldn't say that!)' But by then he was almost at the business end of the room. Guess what the first question was to Dhoni? 'Many people go to Tirupati to offer their hair to the lord. Ever since you took up India's captaincy you've offered your hair little by little to the country's cause. Will we get to see the hair back now that you are no longer captain?'

That was just Sunandan Lele being his jocose self. Dhoni made it clear that while he would stick to the team's needs as a batsman, the hair wasn't coming back ever.

Little did I know that a throwaway comment on my hair would become his customized greeting. A week after the IPL of 2017, we were in England for the Champions Trophy. Nothing had changed in terms of our routine though. India began their campaign in Birmingham against Pakistan. And before I could even say hello as we crossed paths for the first time on English soil, Dhoni went, '*Baal kaat lo, yaar.* (Cut your hair, mate.)'

It was the same at the Oval a few days later as India went back to London for their remaining league matches. He would see me, smile as he got closer and then the same line again. Soon, some of my fellow journalists caught on to it, and would pre-empt his greeting with their own versions of 'baal kaatlo, yaar' when they saw Dhoni approaching. At times I would get a word or two in about how there were other things like the book we could talk about. But he always ended up with the final word. Soon, the Champions Trophy was over, with India losing that famous final at the Oval to Pakistan. Our hair saga was to continue for a few weeks more, that too with new characters joining the cast.

Dhoni and India left for the Caribbean following the Champions Trophy for a three-island tour which involved five ODIs and a solitary T20. So did I. And Dhoni's fixation with getting my hair cut continued. With fewer reporters—the density of media presence had gone from, say, that of Mumbai's western suburbs to the western Australian outback—Dhoni and I did get slightly more time for our sweet nothings. And somehow, almost every conversation started with 'baal kaatlo, yaar'. Dhoni was one of the few cricketers who had his family in tow for the tour. Soon enough, even his wife and daughter joined the anti-hair campaign.

Two-year-old Ziva was first on the job. The Indian team was staying in Antigua at the very posh Sugar Ridge Resort, which has steps leading to the cottages located on a rather steep hill. With the stadium a good forty-minute ride away on Antigua's narrow and unkempt roads, the team management decided to hold the daily press conferences at the hotel itself. I was staying by myself in a desolate part of the island in the north and would generally stay back at Sugar Ridge to finish my daily work. There I would end up witnessing the Indian players, the starry ones included, indulging in rather mundane activities. It ranged from captain Virat Kohli carrying a heavy load of water bottles up to his cottage located on the highest point of the resort to Dhoni ferrying food for his wife and daughter. The latter would walk down with a few empty plastic boxes to the team room, a dining place right outside the lobby, and then appearing a few minutes later with them filled with food.

'*Biwi aur bachche ki seva chalu hai*. (I continue to serve my wife and kid.),' he said, intuitively anticipating my question.

The next time I was there, Dhoni was on babysitting duty and was busy being a doting father to Ziva. And as he carried her back up to their room, Dhoni spotted me. But rather than go for his catchphrase himself, he tried to make Ziva do it. 'Tell him baal kaatlo. Ask him to cut his hair,' he said. Fortunately for me, Ziva either didn't care or perhaps didn't agree with her dad. Sakshi, though, was totally on her husband's side. A few minutes after Dhoni and Ziva had left, she walked into the lobby and was soon asking the media manager, Gaurav Saxena, about the boys. When Gaurav told her that they were fine and Mahi had given me the usual grief, she carefully scanned my hair and then almost immediately said, 'Haan, yaar, I think I want to cut your hair myself.'

'Why is your entire family after my hair? Leave me alone,' I quipped, to which she said, 'Let's fix a date. We'll do it in Jamaica. I'll even get Mahi on the job. It'll be great fun.' 'Yeah, at my expense,' I said. There was a slightly awkward encounter the day after Dhoni had been criticized heavily by everyone, including me, following his bizarrely stodgy 58 off 108 balls with just a single boundary. It was a match where India had fallen 11 runs short of chasing the meagre total of 190 set by a second-string West Indies outfit. Dhoni was undone by a maverick seamer, Kesrick Williams, playing only his second ODI, and the sword over his head had only gotten sharper.

By the time I reached the airport the next morning en route to Jamaica for the final leg of the tour, the Indian team was already making its way in. Desperate to get to the check-in counter before them to avoid the obvious delay, I was rushing through, only to be stopped in my tracks. There stood Mrs Dhoni holding the pram and flashing an ominous smile, while her husband was brandishing an imaginary scissor in my direction. It was also another example of what everyone around Dhoni considers to be his greatest attribute—of being able to 'live in the moment'. It's rare for any sportsperson to look so relaxed and at peace with the world and himself at a time when the axe seems so perilously close to his neck. But that's Dhoni for you.

The gesturing and the taunting continued through the week in Kingston, from all members of the Dhoni family, but somehow they couldn't get to me. As the tour came to an end, I had my final encounter with Dhoni. It, of course, began with the customary 'baal kaatlo, yaar' jibe before I inquired about whether he would be travelling to the USA, which he had done post previous tours to the Caribbean. When asked why he's been so hell-bent on the haircut, he put it down as a matter of practical advice. The way he put it across was very akin to what we hear from him often over the stump camera. I suddenly felt like I was a spinner at the top of my mark, with Dhoni shouting out some prudent order from behind the stumps. 'Don't need to cut it fully. Layering *kara le*. Same length, less weight.'

2

The MECON Boy

'*Paagalkhane ke liye maana jaata tha, sir, Ranchi . . . Kahan ek MECON Colony ke ladke ne hum sab ko aasmaan tak pahuncha diya.* (Ranchi was known mainly for an institution for the mentally ill . . . And from nowhere a boy from the MECON Colony has taken us to the skies.)' You don't have to look or listen too hard to realize that Chittu (Seemant Lohani) is besotted with his Mahi. Chittu is Dhoni's oldest friend—they met at the Dayanand Anglo-Vedic (DAV) Jawahar Vidya Mandir School while still in junior school.

Chittu isn't exaggerating or indulging in loose-tongued hyperbole when he talks about his schoolmate putting Ranchi on the map. It's a fact. Many have likened what Dhoni has done for his home town to what Sir Don Bradman did for his home town, Bowral. But Ranchi is not a sleepy, nondescript town to the south-west of Sydney. It's if anything steeped in Indian history. Once ruled by the Mauryan empire, the people of Ranchi were used to fighting off insurgents, and

11

often with success. They had thwarted the Mughals on one occasion and even gained independence before being recaptured. After the British took over, Ranchi became one of the epicentres of the uprising against colonial rule towards the end of the nineteenth century and was one of the strongholds of the revolutionaries throughout the freedom struggle till 1947. During this time, the district witnessed a number of revolutionary campaigns and anti-British crusades led by Ganesh Chandra Ghosh, the Chittagong-based freedom fighter, who started his own Revolutionary Party. It was in Ranchi that Mahatma Gandhi met the then lieutenant governor of Bihar and Orissa in 1917 regarding the Champaran issue which led to the first-ever satyagraha of any kind in the country.

The city kind of slipped off the national radar in independent India despite being home to ample natural and mineral resources. In the 1990s and well into the new millennium, the region became known for producing a high number of civil service officers and for having a high literacy rate; but then it also had to grapple with innumerable power cuts, where families found it prudent to finish cooking their dinner before the sun set.

But it was Dhoni who firmly put Ranchi on the map again. There is an article online titled 'What Made Ranchi Famous before Dhoni Came Along'. It deals with some of Ranchi's other claims to fame, mostly of yore, including Birsa Munda. Born on 15 November 1875, he was a tribal leader and one of the youngest freedom fighters of that era, whose activism against missionaries and the British left a major impact on India's freedom struggle. The fact that he died when only twenty-five, in a Ranchi jail, puts things in further perspective. He was later honoured with the title of Birsa Bhagwan.

The Ranchi airport is named after Munda, who had even started his own religion. It is said that he did things his own way, often to the bemusement of those around him, much like the man who'd challenge him to the title of Ranchi's most famous son a century later.

Dhoni has himself spoken about the anonymity that his city was engulfed in for years, even as recently as his early days in international cricket. He mentioned this when the JSCA stadium was inaugurated in 2013. It's anybody's guess whether Ranchi could even have dreamt of having its own state-of-the-art ground which would become a regular centre for cricket at the highest level if not for Dhoni.

'When I started my international career, people during the overseas tours used to ask me where I came from. I would first say India, then Jharkhand and then Ranchi. The next question invariably was, "Where is Ranchi?" I had to explain in different ways by saying, "It's near Calcutta, near Jamshedpur from where Tata originated. It's India richest state in terms of minerals. Now the city has its own cricket identity. I can proudly say I'm from Ranchi because of this international stadium,' the *Times of India* quoted Dhoni as saying.[*]

---

[*] Sourav Modak, 'I Can Proudly Say I'm from Ranchi', *Times of India*, 19 January 2013, https://timesofindia.indiatimes.com/england-in-india-2013/top-stories/I-can-proudly-say-Im-from-Ranchi-Dhoni/articleshow/18081847.cms.

Nobody knows Dhoni better than Chittu. This is coming from the man himself. After having waited for him enough times at the MCA stadium, I had eventually given up the ghost and resigned to my fate. Then one day, I thought it better to ask Dhoni himself about how he would have gone about the task of discovering the real Mahi.

Following a dramatic pause, he said, '*Ek hi aadmi hai* . . . Chittu . . . *Lekin woh tujhe milega nahi*. (There's only one man for the job . . . Chittu . . . But he won't meet you . . .),' and then walked away, mouthing something about finding Chittu *naamumkin* (impossible).

A couple of days later, I got a call from an unknown number and the man on the other side introduced himself as Chittu. He said I should come over to Ranchi the very next day. Taken aback, I only got my head around the identity of the caller once I heard the words, '*Mahi ne kaha hai ki aap aaoge*. (Mahi had said that you would come.)'

Flight tickets were booked on the fly and though I couldn't make it as swiftly as Chittu wanted me to, I was in Ranchi the day after.

It would be unfair to say that the Dhoni–Ranchi relationship is one-sided. A lot of why and how Dhoni is the way he is can be traced back to where he comes from, like with most people. 'Our Groundwork Takes You Sky High' is the sign that welcomes you into Ranchi. They couldn't have picked a more apt slogan for the city or its beloved son. It explains both what the city represents and the meteoric rise of

Dhoni. There's an understated yet ambitious air to the city. It remains largely middle class but the real estate is booming with state-of-the-art residential complexes mushrooming on all sides. But still the market area, or Main Road as it's more eloquently referred to there, carries a rather bourgeois feel to it. Though not aggressively advertised, there is enough tourism potential there—it's called the city of waterfalls—to attract visitors in search of the real-India experience.

It is a city, locals believe, that is urbanizing at a rapid pace. Ranchi is a highly cosmopolitan agglomeration—teeming with the educated classes from across the country who came in search of better opportunities post-independence, and migrators from its hinterlands who came in search of jobs, especially after it became the capital of Jharkhand in 2000. It has transformed over the years from being a forest inhabited by tribes to being the administrative headquarters for the British and then to an industrial town with major companies like Bharat Heavy Electricals Limited (BHEL), MECON, Steel Authority of India Limited (SAIL), etc., located there. A considerable change in land use has occurred during the last four decades. Ranchi has been handpicked to become one of the 100 smart cities by the government's Smart City India Mission. This is information I get from a friend who has called Ranchi home for most parts of her life, and is extremely touchy about all things Ranchi.

Chittu has already booked a room for me—or informed the hotel staff—before I land and it's a four-minute car ride from the airport. Hotel Green Acres, like every other place in Ranchi, has its own Mahi memory, and I'm told about it as I check in.

'He used to often come here to our rooftop restaurant with his friends early on. At times, he would even be kind enough to pose for pictures with the staff. Obviously, he doesn't get time to do that very often these days,' the receptionist tells me. The Green Acres' big attraction, apart from its well-kept rooms, is the food—the South Indian food in particular. The hotel itself represents the changing face of Ranchi. It now boasts of its own gourmet patisserie, aptly named Sugar High, which is run by the owner's daughter. There's a Mahi connection here too, of course. Chandrakant Raipat, the owner, went to school with the man himself.

His daughter, Vandita Raipat, who finished her studies in Bangalore and worked briefly in Mumbai before shifting back to her roots to start Sugar High, has her own Dhoni story. It's about the time when she and her friends were cycling around MECON Colony and blocked his car, refusing to budge until he came out and gave them autographs. 'He did eventually step out; he was smiling and gladly posed for pictures with us,' she says. She doesn't sound a tad embarrassed about it. It's Mahi, after all. The people of Ranchi have a legitimate claim on him.

In less than an hour after I check in, Chittu is on his way to meet me. His first look at me is rather incredulous. 'I expected someone much older to be writing a book on Mahi,' he tells me. I could see he was also expecting someone a lot more conventional-looking. Chittu is diminutive, stout and wears thick glasses. The first thought in my head was how perfectly the casting director for *Dhoni—The Untold Story* nailed the Chittu character.

The first thing he does is pull out his phone and insist that I see the McDowell's Soda No. 1 'Yaari Hai' ad that Dhoni had shot with Chittu and Chottu-bhaiya (Paramjit Singh), who was a former clubmate of Dhoni and got him his first sponsor before he became the elder brother of Mahi's inner circle. It's a tastefully shot video that manages to indulge in nostalgia without seeming corny at any point. It used to be on TV till a couple of years ago and the full version is up on YouTube. The camaraderie and intimacy between the three friends is evident in every scene—whether it is Dhoni making fun of Chittu's chai or getting the better of him in an impromptu game of cricket. Dhoni's megastardom isn't compromised, as his friends use a selfie with him as a bait to get a discount from the caterer. Overall, it achieves its purpose perfectly, to depict that the more things change, the more they stay the same. The script, Chittu reveals, was written by Dhoni himself.

The final scene is a touching exchange between the two schoolmates as Chittu speaks wistfully about the good old days and the fun they used to have, to which Dhoni, showing some rare emotion, puts his arms around the two and says, 'Kuch nahi badla, yaar. (Nothing has changed, mate.)' There's also a scene where Dhoni picks on Chittu's slightly generous midriff.

'See how he doesn't let go of that one opportunity he has to make fun of me and my weight. He didn't tell me about it before the shooting began,' he says with a smile and emotion in his voice. As I look up, I also find a glint of a tear or two welling up behind the spectacles. I assume Chittu gets emotional every time he sees the ad.

Being very close to a big-time celebrity in India leaves you in a dangerous state of suspended disbelief. It's a weird drug that few can handle, mainly because you can never be in control of its effects. There are the highs, of course, of getting to rub shoulders with and enjoying a personal relationship with someone who a billion others would give anything to catch a glimpse of. It's also an addictive high but one you are totally dependent on your celebrity friend for providing. You are only important till he or she is. And there's nothing you can do about it. There's also always the overriding fear that the friendship itself could get eclipsed at any point.

Chittu, to his credit, acknowledges the fickleness and responsibilities of being a celebrity confidant. He's tried to keep his personal life divorced from the Dhoni phenomenon that unwittingly engulfs most other facets and faculties of his life. Our chats are repeatedly interrupted by calls from Sakshi who is seeking Chittu's expert opinion on some home matter. The Dhonis are in the process of shifting to their new house in Harmu when I am in Ranchi. And it's the best friend who is the decision-maker when the man is not around. Wherever he goes, he's known as 'Chittu-bhai, Mahi *ka dost*'. He loses his cool briefly when the security guard at the JSCA stadium asks him to move his car from the VIP parking spot, but he doesn't have to throw any names around. The ground incharge is fortunately at hand and he steps in to explain that the guard is a new appointee and therefore not aware of Chittu's identity. But Chittu doesn't impose his celebrity influence over anyone. '*Rehne dijiye, naya hoga.* (Let it be, he must be new.)' He then pats the guard on the back.

We don't hang around the hotel for too long. Chittu can't afford to. He's a busy man when in Ranchi. MECON

Colony will be our first stop, he tells me as we get into his car. It's a Santro. And before I ask, he tells: 'Mahi gave this to me a few years ago. Before this he had given me a Scorpio, the most expensive car I've ever owned. He also had bought me my first bike.' He adds, 'That's why Mahi is special and greater than all other famous cricketers in the world. He doesn't believe in leaving anyone behind. He might have become the biggest celebrity in the country right now. *But woh iss cheez mein manta hai ki sabko saath leke aage chalna hai.* (But he believes in taking everybody forward.)' It's true at many levels, I realize. Though Dhoni has been associated with Rhiti Sports, the sports management company run by Arun Pandey, for years now, he also lets Chittu and a former Jharkhand teammate, Mihir Diwakar, handle his other, newer clients.

And it doesn't take me too long to realize what Dhoni had meant when he talked about his friend's elusiveness.

One of the first things Chittu tells me is that he doesn't do interviews. He keeps a lower profile than even Dhoni in Ranchi. His phone is forever buzzing, but he answers only those numbers that he can recognize. He keeps two phones. One is a private number that only a few—I'm in the illustrious list now—have access to. He tells me how privileged I am—not once but on quite a few occasions. Then a quick reminder: 'I'm meeting you only because Mahi has asked me to. Or I just don't talk to anyone.'

MECON Colony

Dhoni didn't just put Ranchi on the map. He also put MECON Colony on the silver screen and on every television set across the country.

We enter the colony gate with Chittu throwing a customary nod to the security guard. This is after Chittu has shown me Sanjay Tea Stall—located a few metres from the colony gate—which is where the Mahi army would convene on a daily basis once the cricket was over; it has now become one of the many selfie points in Doranda when tourists come here on an M.S. Dhoni tour. It's a modest shop that sells your usual fare of samosas and other basic savouries, along with those customary jeera biscuits that are so characteristic of these shops.

The MECON residential complex in Ranchi, some 5.2 km from the airport in the busy suburb of Doranda, is over sixty years old now and, according to Chittu, hasn't changed much since the time his family moved here. It's a gated community with its evident class hierarchy like most government-owned colonies around the country. The size, wear and tear and overall aesthetics of the many residences give away the financial status of their respective residents.

Chittu takes me on a guided tour of the colony, beginning from the places the two childhood friends used to hang out. Finally, he parks outside the MECON stadium. It's around 6 p.m. and the guard has locked the gate. Chittu flexes his influence and the guard obliges. As we walk in, Chittu takes a whiff of the summer air and smiles. Perhaps it's his way of saying, nothing's changed at all. He immediately starts pointing out the various Mahi landmarks.

'Mahi's family used to stay somewhere in M Block before and then they moved into N Block overlooking the stadium. That was his building, and two blocks behind it was mine,' says Chittu, pointing to his right. He then points straight ahead, beyond the boundary wall at the far end at a clutch of dull-coloured buildings, amidst which the one in white stands out even from a distance. 'That was our school. So we were very lucky that we hardly had to walk five minutes to get there. Behind the school was where Mahi's dad's office used to be. To the left is the pump room where his father would often come to do his work while we would be playing. *Duty yahan tha, ghar wahan, aur school wahan peeche.* (His workplace was there, the house there, and the school behind.)'

It's at this DAV school that Chittu met Mahi while they were still tots. They were polar opposites, but hit it off immediately.

'He was a unique kid. *Ekdum shaant always.* (Always quiet.) I never saw him do kids' stuff, playing pranks or being cranky or throwing tantrums. *Aisa nahi, ki ekdum jhat-pat kuch kar raha hai.* (He never did anything out of the blue.) No *badmaashi* (mischief) either. He was in his own world mostly, almost too sorted to be a child,' says Chittu, adding that even at that young age, what was apparent about Dhoni was a keen sense of knowing what to do, when to do it, and giving it all his focus and energy.

'Very dedicated to his work. If he decided that he had to do something, *woh karna hi hai* (he would definitely do it). He wouldn't study through the year. He would study while the monsoons were on and we couldn't play out much. He wouldn't revise much even when it was exam time. I never saw him mugging up like we used to. It is a first-class brain. Mahi's dad used to come up with this popular dialogue during exam time. "Whoever has studied all year long, doesn't need to study at the last minute. And whoever hasn't studied all year, *usko bhi* last-minute studies *ki zaroorat nahi hai* (he too doesn't have to study at the last minute).'" Wise advice indeed, something you can almost imagine Dhoni using with his bowlers (think S. Sreesanth) often during his captaincy.

The upbringing in both households had a mixture of freedom and discipline. Mahi and Chittu had a curfew to contend with and be back home by 6.30 p.m. regardless of whether they were done playing or not. The adults worked really hard to keep the household going and they expected the kids to do their bit in terms of cultivating self-discipline when it came to school matters.

'After playtime, come back home, wash up and then sit down to study. Everything was fixed for us. Get up early, go to school, play and then study. That's why you'll never see Mahi ever being late to any place. That discipline is so deeply engrained in him,' says Chittu.

Chittu claims to be hot-headed and someone who even now doesn't think twice before getting into a scuffle. 'I was the ultimate *badmaash*, very short-tempered and would keep getting into fights. Even now when Mahi sees me getting angsty with someone, he'll mockingly warn that guy, saying, "Achcha hai. He's running short of enemies at the moment." Despite hanging out with such a cool guy, I have never been able to change that side of me,' he rues.

Dhoni's innate steadfastness would be raised to new levels when it came to sport, says Chittu. It didn't matter what sport he was involved in. It would reveal a new side to Dhoni—one where he would allow himself to show emotion and, at times, even lose his cool. Chittu recalls being Mahi's doubles partner in badminton and the responsibility that came with the role. 'You had to play seriously. That was the only time I would see him get angry. If even for a single point, he felt or got the feeling that I wasn't being as serious as he was, all hell would break loose. "*Khelna hai toh seriously khelo, nahi toh chale jao*. (If you want to play, play seriously; otherwise, go away.)" That was the first warning. The next time he would just shout, "*Bhaag jaao yahan se, tum-mein seriousness nahi hai*. (Get lost from here, you are not serious.)"'

Chittu says that the single-mindedness which Dhoni brought to the task at hand in childhood is evident even today when his friend is busy on the iPad playing one of his beloved shooting games or football. 'He's fully into it, with 100 per cent concentration. But he's still listening to everyone. If anyone thinks even for a second that he's fully fixated on the game and isn't paying attention to what they've said, then they will be in for a shock,' he says with that same awe with which he describes most of Mahi's characteristics.

The MECON stadium is where Mahi and Chittu spent their evenings playing football, and on the odd occasion, some cricket. This was also the only Ranji Trophy venue in Ranchi before the Dhoni phenomenon occurred. And even though cricket was an afterthought most of the time back then, the future India captain would not miss a single ball of the action whenever Bihar was playing a match at the MECON stadium. Sitting on the terrace of N171—his first residence there—the two boys would soak in the Ranji action all day long. It is an envious position to be in—having a first-class ground across the road from you, especially in India. The boy literally grew up with high-level cricket at his doorstep. For most cricketers who make it to the top, especially from the hinterland, the first first-class match they witness is often the maiden one they get to play in.

As Chittu recalls, Dhoni was never a mute spectator—the stump microphone has over the years revealed that he just can't stop talking when a match is on—even back then. He was constantly formulating theories and passing judgements on those playing.

'Bihar used to have a fast bowler called D.J. Singh, and Mahi was always amazed at how quick he bowled. He would keep talking about his pace. Honestly, I wasn't someone who loved discussing cricket for too long, but Mahi would keep at it. It's funny that these days he bashes up bowlers who are much, much quicker than that fellow he used to rave about,' says Chittu with a smile.

Amazingly, it was right here at the MECON stadium that Dhoni made his first-class debut when he was eighteen. He played against Assam and scored an unbeaten 68. When you think of it, it must have been akin to playing your first big-ticket match at the same building compound or gully you learnt to play the sport in. In early 2015, while the World Cup was on Down Under, it was announced that the MECON stadium would be renamed the MECON-MSD stadium in a year's time. But here I am in May 2017, and it still reads MECON stadium, in bold-blue letters. It lacks the MSD touch, quite literally. When asked about it, Chittu just shakes his head, his brows furrowing, but for once he holds back. It's at this precise moment that Umakanta Jena, Jena-da to the locals, joins us.

Umakanta Jena, now well into his sixties, has been the curator at MECON stadium for nearly two decades and was one of the early witnesses to the rise of Dhoni. He's heavily tanned and carries all the signs of long hours spent under the unforgiving Ranchi sun.

And he, like Chittu, is displeased, almost anguished, at the fact that the man who brought MECON and Ranchi such glory does not have his name up there yet. 'Despite all that he's done for the city, the locality and the country, they're yet to give him any recognition. It's been over a year since they publicly announced the renaming of the stadium. But you see, nothing has happened yet,' says Jena-da before recounting his own version of the snub Dhoni received from the 'elitist' MECON team selectors, one that they've never gotten over even if the man himself has moved on.

'*Tabhi bhi nahi samjhe, aur abhi bhi nahi samajh rahe hai ki Mahi hai kya.* (Even in those days they, the powers that be at MECON, did not understand what Mahi was, and even now they don't.),' the veteran curator puts things in perspective. By now, Chittu has 'silenced' at least half a dozen phone calls and when his phone rings yet another time, he turns around and points at one corner of the stadium to the left of the pavilion, and once again simply shakes his head. This time, though, he manages a few words.

'They had promised to turn one section of the MECON ground into a Mahi museum. You have no idea how excited he was,' says Chittu, his finger still pointing towards what looks like a mix of rubble and debris. 'He had even kept his stuff ready to give away, but they never came for it.' Chittu grits his teeth like there's an invective on its way. But nothing. He goes back to shaking his head, now more vigorously than before.

The repeated rebuffs that those close to him lament about have hardly deterred Dhoni from showing up at his literal 'home ground'. He still shows up here whenever he's in town and indulges in some nostalgia, something that he enjoys doing, says Chittu—which, in its own way, is surprising for someone who's celebrated for living in the moment. Jena-da, now smiling, is quick to talk about the last time Dhoni came to the MECON stadium. It was when he was visiting a friend in the colony and heard that there was a junior soccer tournament underway at the venue. Unannounced, he just landed up at the stadium and rather than sit in the office room, plonked himself in the one concrete stand that provides a rather nice viewing experience of the action at the MECON stadium. What followed was an inevitable melee. Like it happens in India so often, thousands appeared literally out of nowhere and the stadium turned into an uncontrollable cauldron. The game, which had continued for a few minutes post Dhoni's arrival, had to be halted, as security guards were called in to clear the crowd. Dhoni had no way out and there were even suggestions made that he jump down from the stands into the parking area—a good 12-feet drop—and make a quick getaway. Sanity prevailed though, and Jena-da insists that Dhoni stayed back and watched the match till it was over and even gave away a few prizes before leaving, in one piece.

Jena-da too has his own recollections of Mahi before he became MSD. He and Dhoni's father, Paan Singh, who moved to Ranchi from his village of Almora in Uttarakhand back in 1964, would play cards together on Sundays and public holidays. Jena-da now stays in the same quarters that Chittu and his mother used to, back in the day. He remembers how Paan Singh was never too appreciative of his son's passion for sports—well documented now in the movie. But while he tried to stay clear of his son's sporting exploits within the colony, Jena-da would catch Paan Singh slyly watching Mahi in action through the grooves on the stadium's boundary wall facing their residence.

'Though his office was behind the school, he would often go to the pump room for some routine work. On his way back, he would quietly go to that corner and watch Mahi bat, and even smile once in a while if he saw his son hit a boundary. He thought nobody knew. But we have known each other for thirty years and I can pick him out from afar. I never bothered him though, I didn't want to ruin his special moment,' says Jena-da.

But Paan Singh, says the curator, didn't appreciate his son compromising on his studies; he disliked Dhoni accepting the never-ending invites to play in tennis-ball cricket tournaments. 'He would get angry, scold him, and come and complain to me. Our card games would be interspersed with his rants about how his (Dhoni's) friends keep coming and taking him away to play in those "canvas-ball tournaments" as he would call them. "That tournament there, this tournament here, the boy shouldn't lose focus on his studies, Jena-da," he would tell me.'" Jena-da would generally just put an arm around the concerned father and tell him that his son was already creating a buzz with his batting feats and that he was made for bigger things.

'That *mahol* (atmosphere) started with just the kids he used to play with. Nobody expected him to go too far. But soon the whole colony was talking about it (his cricketing feats). Before you knew it, everyone wanted a piece of Mahi, and everyone wanted to be part of what they assumed, and correctly so, would be a journey to superstardom, but still not quite like this. The boy would simply not leave the ground, and if it was raining heavily, he would be the first one out with his football,' he says.

Even though this is peak summer, the light fades fast in the east of India. Chittu wants us to get going so that we can take a few pictures of the colony before it's too late. As he's about to leave, Jena-da taps him on the shoulder and whispers something into his ear. It's something to do with him not receiving payment for a job he'd done at another ground. Chittu pacifies the old man and tells him that it'll be done. It's a role that Chittu ends up playing wherever he goes—that of the proxy agent, caretaker and problem-solver for pretty much everyone close to Dhoni. And he does it well.

We are now right outside N171 where Dhoni grew up. There are a few kids playing cricket in the gully parallel to the building. Chittu politely asks them to continue with the game as it would enhance my photograph of the place. Understandably, the batsman, who'd till then been trying to pierce the tiny gap between the two fielders on the off-side, now wants to only attempt the helicopter shot. He has, of course, been informed about the purpose of my visit and the boy knows exactly whose former house he's batting next to.

'Some trivia for you,' says Chittu, pointing at the building, 'you know he used to stay on the first floor, but when they were shooting for the movie they couldn't get a good shot of that house from here. So, we convinced the residents on the second floor, above what was Mahi's home, to allow us a few days to shoot at their house.' Chittu should know. He was the unofficial consultant for the movie and spent hours and days with the scriptwriters and director, taking them around the many points of interest in Ranchi, including the MECON Colony.

N171 was a two-room house with one wall covered with Sachin Tendulkar posters, thanks to the young boy who grew up dreaming of one day playing cricket for his country. This love and immense respect for Tendulkar never faded away even after Dhoni took over as Indian captain and, technically, had his idol play under him. 'On the field, Dhoni was always the captain. Tendulkar might suggest a bowling change to him, ask him to bring on a spinner, but Mahi would tell him politely that it wasn't a great idea, and would stick to his plan of keeping the fast bowler going. He always remained the General. But if Mahi ever saw Sachin walking towards him in a hotel lobby, he would always instinctively give way. That was out of genuine respect and he never ever was faking it,' says one close confidant of Dhoni.

And how can we forget the mobile guard of honour that Dhoni instigated at the Wankhede stadium in November 2013 on Tendulkar's final moments as an international cricketer. There's a fascinating episode narrated to me by someone quite close to both wherein Sakshi wanted Tendulkar's autograph before his final Test in Mumbai. And despite being captain, Dhoni kept dilly-dallying, but Sakshi had had enough. It was the night before the match—Tendulkar's 200th and final Test, against the West Indies at the Wankhede—and the Dhonis ended up outside Sachin's room after much deliberation, with Dhoni insisting it wasn't a great idea to disturb him. He waited for a couple of minutes before knocking, and once Sachin opened the door and asked them to come in, Dhoni is believed to have rather sheepishly said, 'Sorry, Sachin, she wants your autograph on this shirt. *Aap jaldi de do* (You please give it to us quickly), and we'll be off.' Despite Tendulkar's insistence that the two should come in, Dhoni had his way and Sakshi the autograph.

The Dhoni family moved out of N171 in 2005—the year he scored those two breathtaking ODI centuries, including the highest score for a wicketkeeper in 50-over cricket, 183 not out against Sri Lanka at Jaipur—and into a bigger house within the colony. It was an individual house with a garden at the back. And this is our last stop as the light has all but faded. Meanwhile, Chittu has already set up my next meeting. It's with Keshav Lal Banerjee, the man who turned Dhoni into the cricketer we all know, or, as Chittu puts it, 'The only cricket coach Mahi has ever had.'

3

The Portrait of a Cricketer as a Young Boy

It's been around ten minutes since Chittu and I walked into the vast premises of the DAV school. Like the rest of the city, DAV is an interesting blend of now and then. The main school building itself is two-storey high. It's a modular concrete building with perforated screens and tiled roofs. What catches my eye though are the many open spaces around, not a sight that metro cities offer. The bracket-shaped building allows for plenty of space in the middle for the kids to indulge in a variety of activities. It also turns into a mini-auditorium whenever their most famous alumnus shows up as chief guest for a function. The premises are big enough to have a number of gated entrances at various vantage points around the school. Our entry is through Gate No. 3. It's the month of May and it's the holiday season. But there is still some activity as kids walk in and out carrying their badminton racquets. The air is pleasanter here than outside, thanks to the handsome smattering of green on all sides.

Around the back is where the cricket nets are. The sun has more or less set completely over the MECON Colony but I still find a young man—a potential batting star in the making, according to my guide, Chittu—in full gear facing throwdowns from another boy who looks younger than him. The setting is quiet enough for the thud of willow on leather to echo around the area. It's in the midst of this impressive display that I first come across Banerjee sir.

I hear Banerjee sir before I see him. He's much older than his pictures suggest but has retained a stable gait and a strong posture. There's every bit of the sports master about the man. I'm soon escorted to the school premises and a security guard is asked to unlock the door to the principal's office. 'He (the principal), like most of the kids, is away on vacation. So we can use his room,' says Banerjee. I'm welcomed into a room—with wooden showcases, chairs and a wide desk—which is just so prototypically a principal's office that it gives me a few nostalgic shudders about the many visits that I have made to this esteemed section at my own school. Before we begin, he apologizes again for having kept me waiting.

It is difficult to imagine Keshav Ranjan Banerjee having ever been a hard man when you look at him now. So when he talks about the tough time he gave M.S. Dhoni and his school team after they lost a must-win game, I simply can't believe him, or maybe I don't want to. The story goes that DAV school were up against what their long-standing coach describes as a '*faaltu*' (useless) team in a league match. Dhoni was among the senior boys in the team, and they ended up losing the match. It wasn't so much the loss that irked Banerjee. He recalls the boys having taken it a tad easy against the underdogs and being lacklustre in their approach.

'I was irate. I was very upset too. As they walked off the field, I shouted at them, insisting that only the younger members of the team would be allowed to get on to the bus, and the senior boys, including Mahi, would have to walk back to the school or wherever they wanted to go. The bus would leave without them,' Banerjee recalls. True to his word, the coach and the kids left with the bus, leaving Mahi and company stranded. The ground was in Harmu—where Dhoni now lives—which was a good 6 km away from the school. It was a warm summer's day and the boys had already felt the brunt of the unforgiving sun on the field.

Still seething, but now slightly concerned about the boys, Banerjee waited at the school gate for the boys to return. Around half hour later, he spotted them trundling up the road with Mahi in the lead. He still remembers Mahi's face all too vividly. It was placid as ever and there was even a hint of a smile as he spotted his coach from a distance.

'I'm sure they took a lift. The ground was quite far. It was a punishment, but more importantly, I wanted them to realize what they had done. I wanted to see how they would react to this. Mahi didn't flinch or even have a frown on his face. Most kids will react. But he was the main player. And clearly, he'd asked the rest to simply follow his lead. Nothing has changed about him even now,' recalls Banerjee. Thinking back, the coach admits to having been a tad worried about the repercussions of his radical lesson on discipline.

'You never know. I was half expecting some *pitaji* (a dad) to come and complain to me the next day, saying, "So what if they lost a game. How could you leave my son stranded, and make him walk so far in the sun?" But nobody came.' It was only much later that Banerjee found out through one of the boys that Mahi had told his teammates to keep the issue under wraps and not inform the parents.

'Of all the boys he was the only one to realize exactly why I had not allowed them on the bus,' Banerjee says with a smile. The way he would do over and over again as an international cricketer, here too, Dhoni had analysed the situation in front of him with a calm mind. Instead of panicking, he had found a solution to it—hitching a ride and also ensuring that the purpose behind his coach's exercise wasn't wasted, which it would have been if even one of his teammates had informed the parents. Dhoni had learnt his lesson, and along the way, also revealed something vital about himself to Banerjee.

Some two decades later, the coach recalls this incident as one of the prime reasons he's always felt with great conviction that '*Mahi hamesha sabse hatke tha, aur hamesha hatke rahega.* (Mahi was always different from every one, and will always remain so.)'

He doesn't stop there. 'I come across nearly 4000 to 5000 kids a day at school. In my career, I've seen some 60,000 to 70,000 walk in through those gates, grow up in front of my eyes and then walk out. But none have walked in like Mahi did, and none have walked out like he did,' Banerjee asserts.

Banerjee sir isn't an elusive man like Chittu. He was originally a sports teacher in Kolkata before shifting to Ranchi a year after Dhoni joined DAV in kindergarten. He does interviews, quite often too. But he doesn't generally delve too deeply into a summation of his favourite student's personality. This is different though, he tells me. Mahi himself has given the go-ahead. Seated to my right, Chittu nods in agreement, followed by a reiteration.

'There are a lot of people who claim to have been responsible for the Mahi phenomenon. Some claim to be mentors, others claim to be coaches. But, according to me and Mahi himself, he's had only one coach, and that's sir,' Chittu says, pointing at the elderly gentleman seated on the other side of the wooden desk. Banerjee flashes a shy smile in response and reveals with pride how his former pupil had told those making the Dhoni movie that there was only man responsible for playing cupid between him and cricket.

The start of Dhoni's affair with cricket has been well documented over the years. Long before Sushant Singh Rajput and Rajesh Sharma added a dollop of Bollywood flavour to how Banerjee transformed a football-crazy goalkeeper into the most successful wicketkeeper batsman in Indian cricket history, it had already become one of the most popular tales of sporting discoveries of our times. But the coach doesn't mind repeating it one more time for my benefit.

Perhaps the most fascinating part of how Banerjee and Dhoni came across each other for the first time is how clichéd it is. It's a scene played out almost every year in every school around the country. A desperate coach suddenly in need of some players as his main ones approach the dreaded black hole of their school sports careers—the tenth to twelfth standard phase. Banerjee's need was dire. He needed to fill a vacancy that required a long-term candidate. DAV's wicketkeeper at that point happened to be in Class XI and with less than a year of school cricket left in him.

Wicketkeepers are like good bassists for a metal band. They're difficult to find, and when you do find a good one, you never want to let him go. Banerjee didn't have much time left. 'Academics always got precedence over sport here, and once a kid was in twelfth, *khel-kood bandh* (no more sports). That's it. No questions asked. I couldn't just go and say, "*Chod ke aao.* (Leave that and come.)" I was sick and tired of finding wicketkeepers in the eighth or ninth standards and then having to let them go after a couple of years. Mahi was in sixth then. And I just dragged him in. He was the perfect fit in so many ways,' Banerjee says.

There's an unbridled joy you see in Dhoni whenever he's involved in a game of football. It's different from what we get to see on the cricket field. He even reacts a lot more. He might finish off ODIs and T20s with a last-over six and nonchalantly walk off like it's just business as usual; but he celebrates almost every goal he scores in the mandatory football matches that the Indian team indulges in at the start of every practice session. And you'll never see him miss out on any opportunity to show off his striking skills in the celebrity football matches that are usually played in Mumbai.

Even back when Banerjee had turned him from goalkeeper to wicketkeeper, Dhoni's love for football didn't suffer. The coach recalls him playing football for the school regularly till around the tenth standard. And Banerjee never stopped him either.

'He used to have football shoes in his bag always, and when cricket practice would be called off due to heavy rains, he would go and play football. I never stopped him like some coaches would say, "No, no, you're a cricketer."'

Banerjee is an old-school coach in all other respects though. He abhors the practice of parents carrying kitbags and accompanying their kids to practice. He doesn't appreciate them interfering in their children's sport. Before becoming a coach, he was a teacher. He always believed that kids needed to learn how to fend for themselves.

'If a child walks out of the school and his parents are waiting for him with the car, he won't learn anything. Let the kid walk to the school by himself rather than getting dropped off daily. If he gets late, he should know school *mein late aane se kya punishment hoti hai* (what punishment awaits him for being late). This is the struggle,' Banerjee explains.

'He Doesn't Fear Failure'

It's no wonder that Banerjee saw in Dhoni a perfect fit. For, it was not just when he graced the international arena that Dhoni became the foremost pragmatist of his generation, he'd always been one, as coach Banerjee recalls. It helped that he also had a coach as pragmatic as he was. Banerjee insists that Dhoni embraced the struggle, rather than fighting it or shying away from it. It's something he continues to do.

'It's not like they were ever short of money or food. Mahi's struggle was different. In those days, most kids didn't own their own kits. We had to manage. These days, mummy, papa will buy full flashy kit for their kids, and they'll come, sit and watch them all day long. Those days, at the most you had your own water bottle. Mahi enjoyed the grind of becoming a sportsman. He thrived on it. *Struggle se aadmi seekhta hai.* (A person learns through struggle.) It teaches you to take decisions,' says Banerjee.

Another aspect of Dhoni's personality—one that has left the cricket world in awe—which impressed Banerjee rather early was the ability to shake off every external element, including the trappings of fame, while he was in the middle.

'Mahi is still learning his craft. He never stops learning. Sometimes I see him and I'm reminded of the sixth-standard boy whom I met all those years ago. The eagerness to learn, which can be seen in his eyes, has never dimmed. Most kids at that age will play one or two tournaments, score a few runs here and there and start showing off like they know everything there is to know about the sport. Mahi never showed off even then. *Practice toh practice, match toh match, koi dikkat nahi hai.* (If it's practice, it's going to be practice. Same with matches. No confusion.)'

Dhoni brought the same attitude even to his academics. Though Banerjee wasn't ever directly involved with his star student's studies, he remembers one visit to the Dhoni household very vividly. That was when Mahi's mother pulled up the coach and gave him a piece of her mind.

'She had some stern words for me,' he says with a guffaw. 'She said, "If his marks and studies suffer, I will not spare you."'

But Dhoni himself was never too stressed by the task of managing his cricket and studies. The term 'exam fever' never existed in the Dhoni book, says the coach. Even during the exam season, if anyone was to call him for a match, Dhoni would write the exam and then go to play. And not just any exam—he did so even during his Class XII exams. Banerjee still shakes his head in disbelief when he recalls one particular incident. With the mother's threat still very much in his mind, the shocked coach approached Mahi to find out if he was actually serious about going to Orissa to represent his club, Central Coal Limited (CCL), in a league match in between the board exams.

'I told him, "This is not an internal exam. That we can manage. These are your boards. *Beta*, aren't you worried?" He said, "Sir, pass *ho jaaonga main* (I will pass), don't worry." 'The board exam started at 10 a.m. DPS Ranchi was the centre; 1 p.m. it finished. The CCL car was waiting for him from 11.30 itself with his kit and bag. He got out, changed from his school clothes, got into the car and headed straight to the station to take the train. You get a two-day gap between papers during the boards. He returned after two days, started studying and went and took the exam the following day.' Dhoni ended up scoring somewhere between 55–60 per cent in his twelfth-standard exams where commerce was his main subject. Incidentally, a lot of his friends who 'studied day and night', say both Chittu and Banerjee, fared no better.

'Mahi never stressed too much about studies. His sister would often go to one of his classmates' house to get his notes sorted since he had missed classes due to cricket,' Banerjee reveals.

Dhoni's style of studying, like every other aspect of him, was unique. The night before the exam, his sister would read the notes out aloud while he closed his eyes and listened. That was all he needed. Banerjee isn't too surprised about how Dhoni approaches run chases in limited-overs cricket. He's seen him employ the same 'cool as ice' demeanour to the examinations he faced off the field.

'He realized that the more tense you are, the more nervous you get and your performance gets affected. He employs the same mindset to everything in life. Exam and cricket *ka* funda are the same. If out *ho gaye, toh* out. So, why fret about it before it happens. He doesn't fear failure. That's where this innate confidence comes from,' says Banerjee.

And Dhoni's incredible self-confidence seems to have nothing to do with whether things were going his way or not. Banerjee remembers that his ward was as confident as ever even during some of the lowest points in his life. One of them came early in his career, just around the time he had started making a name for himself on the domestic circuit and had even earned a call-up to the national camp in Chandigarh. Back then in 2001, Dhoni was competing against Deep Dasgupta and Ajay Ratra for a spot in the India A squad. A stint at the national camp alongside the best players in the country would have given him a vital first-hand glimpse at the level he was working so hard to reach. Unfortunately, Dhoni fractured his wrist and had to give the trip a miss. Banerjee found himself in the difficult position of checking on Mahi's morale and making sure that the youngster didn't take the blow too badly.

'I asked him, *"Tum jaaoge nahi?* (You won't go?)" I couldn't say anything negative to him in that state. I was worried whether he'll get another chance. It's always tricky for a wicketkeeper. And that was the time India had found a number of them, some even younger than Mahi. But he was the one who told me, "Don't worry, sir. I know I'll get one more chance, you just wait and see, and I'll take that chance." That was the kind of unbelievable confidence he had in himself,' Banerjee says with a wide smile.

An emotion that Banerjee claims to have never seen in Dhoni is that of anger or frustration. This, despite all the trials and tribulations he underwent before his star began to rise. There was the snub from the MECON selectors. But that was not all. There was always an obstacle to overcome and always a detractor to be proved wrong. But while Dhoni rode through them with as much equanimity as ever, it was often painful for his support crew, the likes of Chittu, coach Banerjee and Chottu-bhaiya.

'Whether it was with SAIL, CCL, Railways, Ranji or India A, there was always some issue he had to deal with.

I remember at South Eastern Railway, some players didn't want Mahi to bat higher up the order, because they were scared he would score runs and progress past them. He already had a reputation of being a big hitter. But he never protested,' chimes in Chittu, who had so far sat tending to the many messages on his two phones.

'Mahi's nature is that he doesn't do bad things to anybody. Even if someone wrongs him in any way, the worst Mahi will do is stop talking to them. *Door rehta hai, lekin bolega nahi ki tum galat ho.* (He stays away from them, but will never say they are wrong.) If he gets angry, nobody can stand in front of him. It's true when they say those who get angry rarely are the scariest when they do. Luckily, only Sakshi and I get to see that side of him,' Chittu laughs before holding his ears and shaking his head, with his tongue sticking out.

Almost on cue, Chittu receives a call and excuses himself. He promises to meet me later that night to continue our exploration of the world of Mahi, and takes leave of Banerjee with a quick joke.

'Some guys are just talkative. Chittu is talkative,' quips Banerjee as soon as his ex-student leaves the office. Then the topic slides back to Mahi without any prompting.

'Mahi was never talkative. He's a "write the answer to the point" kind of guy. Shy, almost an introvert. He always preferred the outdoors though and would make sure he sat next to a window in class. The primary class kids would be playing and he would keep observing them,' says Banerjee. That would often be mistaken for daydreaming, and was the only time Dhoni would be pulled up by a teacher. Those

around him put it down to this insatiable need to o
and learn something new.

I saw it for myself during IPL 2017 as he and Australian captain Steve Smith spent a good half hour grappling with a drone camera at the end of a practice session at the MCA stadium in Pune. The first fifteen minutes of fiddling was rather random, and not surprisingly, it was Dhoni—Mr Gadget to those around him—who cracked the code and had the drone flying.

I share this with Banerjee and he cites an example of his own to highlight just how good Dhoni's power to grasp any new skill is. 'I had a scooter back in the day. I used to bring my son for practice those days. He was a little boy and one day he got hit on the leg by a stray shot that went in his direction. He was crying and needed to be taken home. I couldn't leave the practice session. I asked Mahi if he would go. He agreed. "But I have a scooter, how will you go?" He said, "Give me the keys." I looked at him with a bemused look on my face and asked, "*Sab chalana aata hai?* (Do you know to ride everything?)" He replied, "*Bike toh aa gaya hai. Scooter bhi aa jaayega.* (I know how to ride a bike. I'll figure out how to ride a scooter too.)" And just like that, he comfortably rode my scooter home. That was only through observing me all those years. To my knowledge, he had never ridden a scooter before.'

Dhoni's quiet yet affable nature also made him really popular in school and in the dressing room. He would never say much but when he did, he would either have those around him in splits or make them sit up and notice.

'He would respect everyone, so he got respect back. That's the way he plays. *Khelke respect lene mein and senior bolke respect lene mein farak hai.* (There's a difference in gaining respect through your game, and gaining it by merely being a senior.),' says Banerjee.

This was the time Dhoni started wearing full-sleeved shirts while keeping wickets. While the full sleeve invokes derisive looks on the field when it comes to a bowler—considering its association with bowlers with dodgy actions—in Dhoni's case, it was once again a practical move. There was one match in particular in Jamshedpur when the harsh sun and dry heat during the summer burnt the hair on his arms. It was to prevent this that Dhoni turned to covering his arms completely while behind the stumps, a practice that became a habit which continues to this day.

Then there was a match in 1997 where Dhoni, a Class X student, insisted on opening and got his way; it was the innings that Banerjee considers the turning point of his career. It was on an important day, an inter-school final. Dhoni ended up scoring an unbeaten 213 and shared a 378-run stand with Shabir Husain for the first wicket. That was the innings which brought him his first professional contract with the CCL. But if Banerjee had had his way, it might not have turned out quite like that.

'The inter-school matches used to be played on matting. So, opening was not a great idea for him. We preferred him at (No.) four because that's where most runs came from in those matches. He would walk out by the eighth or the ninth over and the ball would have lost its shine. The ball would then keep low and allow him to hit *fatafat*, which was his style even back then. Plus this was a final. So I was really worried,' says Banerjee. But Dhoni was adamant despite his coach warning him about the peril the team would be in if he made that one mistake against the moving ball and got out early. Eventually, upon realizing that Dhoni was going to have his way, Banerjee caved in but only on one condition.

'I will not make anyone pad up. Not even the No. 3. If you go there, you have to finish it. I wanted to change his playing habit. If you open, you have to change your style of playing. I don't even remember whether I stood by my word and stopped the No. 3 from padding up. We didn't need him. Those two finished off the run chase without losing a wicket,' says Banerjee.

'That was the turning point. I just sat on the sidelines and watched in amazement. That innings proved to me that he'll play for India.' Banerjee's eyes twinkle as if he can still see it in front of his eyes two decades later.

Banerjee, incidentally, wasn't the only one at DAV to foresee the superhuman rise of Dhoni. There was someone else too, and she wasn't even at the ground to witness that blitzkrieg. She was one of Dhoni's classmates. Banerjee still sounds flabbergasted while talking about her.

'I had gone to his class to call him for a match. The teachers would create a fuss if I sent another kid. It was an "accounts" lecture in eleventh or twelfth standard.' The teacher in class that day was Sharmistha Kumar, who taught business and accounts. Later in the staff room, it was Kumar who would tell Banerjee about her encounter with the unlikely Nostradamus.

'So, apparently, as soon as Mahi and I left, one girl suddenly got up, and said, "Ma'am, don't let him go. Take his autograph before you let him go. You won't get it later on." I told her but who knows when or if he'll play for India. Later on, when Mahi was picked for India, one of the first people I thought of was that girl who foresaw his rise before anyone else,' says Banerjee.

I wondered aloud whether Banerjee sir would have even noticed Dhoni if he wasn't a sportsman, that is, considering his unassuming disposition. The veteran coach almost dismisses the thought, saying he couldn't ever picture Mahi as a non-sportsman, since that's all he saw the boy doing from the first time they met—play sport.

We are interrupted a couple of times as the peon knocks on the door asking for the keys to the badminton court. It is summer-camp time and the kids training for badminton have arrived for the evening session. The mention of the badminton court immediately evokes more Mahi talk.

'He obviously can't come as often as before but whenever he does, I know the only place in school that he wants to visit. That's the badminton court. So, we lock the whole premises and sneak him in. Chittu or one of his other friends will show up and he'll be on the court for hours on end,' says the coach. Dhoni was the head boy of the school in the sports category for a couple of years, but Banerjee says he could have been the overall head boy too, such was his reputation.

And Sharmistha Kumar, the accounts teacher, agrees. In an interview to the *Telegraph*, she had said, 'He spent a lot of time on the field, playing cricket, and when he came to class, I used to ask him, "My God, Dhoni, you have missed so many classes. What you will do now?" And he used to say, "Ma'am, you tell me how I can cope with my studies and my cricket given the limited time." Any teacher was ready to help him because he was so polite and humble.' She had also spoken about how all the teachers had pitched in to help Dhoni clear his final examination, and praised him for being a kid who 'never indulged in gossip'.*

What also endeared Mahi to his school teammates was his willingness to go the extra mile to ensure his team did well in every tournament it participated in. At times, it meant double duty for him, as by then he had already started playing for the CCL in the 1997–98 season. And on the days when school and club matches clashed, there would often be a mini tug-of-war between the coaches of both teams. The CCL would obviously get its way since Dhoni was a professional there, even as Banerjee tried everything to get his way.

'Our school team depended totally on four or five players, including Mahi. We used to manage somehow without him. There was one situation when there was an important match for both teams on the same day. The CCL secretary was the district secretary. I requested him to let go of Mahi. I told him they have other big players in their office team. But not having Mahi leaves a huge hole in

---

* Arti Sahuliyar, 'School Basks in Dhoni Glory', *Telegraph*, 4 December 2004, https://www.telegraphindia.com/1041204/asp/ranchi/story_4086323.asp.

my team. *Jaane dijiye usse.* (Leave him for us.) He said no, we can't play without him. Then I asked Mahi. He said, "*Haan, hum khelenge* (Yes, I'll play) if the school match is pushed back by a day." I said, "*Lekin*, two days mein two matches in this heat?" He said, "*Teen khel loonga, sir.* (I can play three, sir.)"' Unlike with club matches, playing for the school meant carrying your team kit, etc., and if you got injured, the first-aid had to be done by yourself. But Dhoni never made a fuss. And the fact that his team won more often than not when he was around, only added to his growing popularity.

That Dhoni has managed to maintain his humility throughout doesn't surprise Banerjee. The two meet often whenever the superstar is in town, and the coach has visited his pupil's house on a few occasions. The junior Banerjee—whom Dhoni had scootered home as a teenager—is close to him and gushes about his Mahi-bhaiya. The coach says they share mutual respect and despite Dhoni's meteoric rise, the equation between the two has not changed.

'A lot of people tell me, "*Dhoni se maangte kyun nahi ho, money and gifts*? (Why don't you ask Dhoni for money and gifts?)" A student–teacher relation is very different. *Guru dakshina nahi poochna chahiye.* (A guru should not ask for any offering from his disciple.) The only thing I ask of him is to keep performing at his best or at times to win the World Cup,' says Banerjee.

The coach believes that his ward has not made too many changes to his game. There was one particular quirk in his wicketkeeping that still amuses Banerjee. But we'll come to that later in another chapter. The swivel hook and the cross-batted slog that Dhoni has mastered over the years come naturally to him, says the one who has seen the man at close quarters since his schooldays. As for Dhoni's innate sense to pick length and his hawk-like hand-eye coordination, the coach puts that down to batting a lot on the ground next to the school gate.

'There are small and big stones on that ground. There was no point in removing all the stones; it would have taken forever. So, we would put a mat on top of those stones and play. You could never be sure how the ball would behave. One would come to your ankles while the next would fly past your ear,' recalls Banerjee. So, when Dhoni would practise his batting on this ungainly and awkward surface, he would simply focus on playing across the line. He would play a hook or pull shot to every ball that came his way.

'If it stayed low, he hooked it, if it rose high, he hooked it,' Banerjee relates laughingly. 'That's how he broke all the window panes on that one side of the school, and I was summoned routinely to the same room we're sitting right now, by the principal. While in international cricket, bowlers are more often than not bowling short of a length intentionally to thwart Dhoni's attacking prowess, it was while contending with this pinball-board–like surface that the right-hander developed the ability to react to the ball rather than focus on any other factor around.

As regards the power his disciple generates, Banerjee puts it down to his pahari origins. 'He always had powerful arms. Pahari people are generally strong mentally and physically. They're used to going up and down (the hill trail), and in Mahi's case, *woh khaata bhi bahut tha* (he used to eat a lot). Back then, he would eat whatever he got. Now he's a raja. He can eat whatever he wants. *Dildaar hai khaane mein!* (He has a voracious appetite!)'

Chittu says that's no longer the case. '*Aaj kal toh sirf grilled chicken khata rehta hai.* (These days he only eats grilled chicken.) He wants to play that 2019 World Cup and he's ready to do anything for that. He's the fittest that I've ever seen,' he says. Chittu too says that food has always played an important role in Dhoni's life.

'It was very simple for Mahi. The days his team won anything, he would celebrate it with chicken. He loves chicken,' says Chittu. Dhoni's Twitter profile says that he is 'perennially hungry for chicken butter masala'. Chittu recalls the morning when Dhoni was selected to the Indian team for the first time. Dhoni was in Jamshedpur and he arrived at around 8.30 a.m. with mithai. Then he picked up all his friends in the Black Scorpio that had by then become synonymous with him around Ranchi. And off they went to the all-day dhaba on the outskirts which had always been their traditional late-night haunt. There are no prizes for guessing what the order was. 'Chicken butter masala, of course,' says Chittu.

Now, there was only one more person in Dhoni's inner circle that I had to meet—Chottu-bhaiya. We were to meet the next afternoon at a common spot before he took me to his now-famous sports-goods shop, Prime Sports, on his bike.

Chottu-bhaiya picked me up from our preordained spot and off we went. But before we could get there, he suddenly stopped the bike, turned around and started laughing. Slightly taken aback but still taken in by his boisterous and infectious laugh, I too joined in, albeit with a puzzled look on my face. Noticing my obvious bewilderment, he said, '*Arré,* I never thought I would be taking around a long-haired guy on a bike around Ranchi again. And that too a guy who's come to write a book on our Mahi.'

4

Prime Time

Ravindra Jadeja recently revealed that Dhoni owns forty-three or forty-four bikes.[*] It's not his fault that he couldn't come up with a precise number. For, according to the all-rounder, Dhoni himself often loses count of how many vaunted two-wheelers there are in his garage. A couple of years ago, Dhoni's vehicular worth was set at twenty-three bikes and ten cars. And the collection included brands that the average Indian hears of only in the movies—Ducati, Harley-Davidson and even one that sounds and looks like something that Batman would own, the Confederate X132 Hellcat.

---

[*] G. Krishnan, 'You Will Never Believe How Many Bikes MS Dhoni Owns', DNA, 12 July 2017, http://www.dnaindia.com/cricket/report-you-will-never-believe-how-many-bikes-ms-dhoni-owns-2500079.

Chhotu-bhaiya, though, remembers Mahi knocking on his door one morning and asking whether he would lend him his RX 100, India's own racer bike from the 1990s. Dhoni then didn't have a bike of his own. The two first met at the Royal Club in 1995 where Chhotu was a senior player and Dhoni the talented upstart. Since Chhotu had a bike, which he'd bought a year earlier, the coach had requested him to pick up and drop the shy and quiet kid from his home inside the MECON Colony. It was during these bike rides, despite lengthy periods of silence, says Chhotu, that the two began developing a unique bond.

'His friends were going to Hazaribagh (known for its sanctuary and forests) on a biking trip. But they were leaving Mahi behind since he didn't own a bike. He came to me and said, "Bhaiya, bike *dena*, please,"' he recalls. Hazaribagh is a 95-km, three-hour ride from Ranchi. While Chhotu had no qualms about lending the bike—considering how well-versed Mahi was with riding it—there was one issue.

'The lights weren't working for some reason. I asked him to take the bike but return before sunset since it would be risky without the lights. He said, "Don't worry, I'll be back before it gets dark." They, of course, didn't return before eleven or twelve in the night, and I and a friend nearly went half the distance looking for them,' he says. And Chhotu wasn't surprised to find Mahi comfortably gliding on the empty roads, more confidently than those with perfectly working headlights.

'The tension, as always, was all mine. He looked as cool as ever,' he adds.

While Dhoni's *chaska* (liking) for two-wheeler rides is well documented, it was on Chhotu's RX 100 that he first indulged in it before he could afford one himself. It was also this RX 100 that witnessed the coming together of two people who became really close friends, who have never let the age difference come in the way. Chhotu says, '*Chaska toh pehle se tha. Lekin bike se pyaar meri RX 100 pe hi hua.* (He had this liking for bikes, but it all began on my RX 100).'

History repeated itself a couple of years ago, as Dhoni, though not quite directly, came asking for Chhotu's RX 100 again. It was the Dhoni filmmakers who wanted to borrow it, and once again Chhotu readily handed over his prized possession. The lights were in working condition this time around.

Chhotu pauses suddenly and then informs me that I too had just become a part of history. 'Sir, the bike that I picked you up on is that exact same RX 100,' he says with a hearty laugh.

'Mahi's first bike was an RX 135, a more powerful bike than mine. But he never got to ride it much, and sold it off rather early,' Chhotu adds. For the record, Dhoni had tweeted a picture of what he called his 'first bike', a Rajdoot which he got restored in 2013. But I'm nobody to challenge Chhotu-bhaiya's version of Mahi's history with two-wheelers.

Then came the fancy bikes, one after the other; there was also the Batmobile on two wheels. Chittu, not much of a biker himself, shares another biking tale. Once, he was allowed to ride one of Dhoni's high-end bikes, but unfortunately, he fell down with it. After the incident, Chittu remembers approaching Dhoni ashen-faced and embarrassed. 'But the first thing he said was, "*Tumko chot nahi lagi, na? Bike toh ban jaayegi.* (You are not hurt, right? The bike can be fixed.)"' That's supposed to be another instance, and there were many I heard in Ranchi, of how Dhoni still remains rooted and cares for the people who've stuck with him on this amazing ride.

Chittu hasn't joined us for this midday chat near the busy Sujata Chowk, which is abuzz with people and activity. Prime Sports is the kind of sports-goods store that has more or less gone extinct in cities like Mumbai and Delhi; you might find the odd mom-and-pop version of a sports store still standing in the suburbs, but most of urban India has moved on to the Decathlons of the world. Prime Sports is a throwback to the 1990s, when sports-goods stores were like any other where the customer stood on one side of the counter and trusted the shopkeeper to get exactly what was needed. There was no question of self-service. The cramped space inside Prime is packed with boxes and cartons stacked on top of each other, while the glass shelves are filled with sundry items, including a number of unmarked trophies for sale—again, things that you don't get to see in modern-day sports stores.

Prime Sports, which Chottu owns, is also an unofficial shrine to a man who once spent many hours within its confines. The side shelf, the one facing the busy road, is filled with screenshots of Dhoni's first foray into Indian cricket's public consciousness—his brutal exploits on an India A tour to Kenya, which included the two centuries against Pakistan A which propelled him to the national team in three months' time.

Chhotu happily provides a guided tour to all comers, and does it every bit like a museum curator, to the extent of corroborating every anecdote about Mahi with corresponding pictures or newspaper cuttings—right from the time he was anonymous even in Ranchi to becoming one of the most well-known faces in Indian sport around the world. The first picture he points to is of a fresh-faced Dhoni looking rather pleased with his brand-new sweater and wicketkeeping gloves. It's from the morning of his Ranji Trophy debut for Bihar at the MECON stadium on 12 January 2000 against Assam.

The Dhoni journey is surreal at various levels. I tell Chhotu about how Dhoni's face has hardly changed, and the hair is a lot like how it is now without being stylized. *'Sir, aadmi change nahi hua hai, face kaise change hoga?* (Sir, when the man himself has not changed, how can his face?),' he shoots back, laughing. There's another one next to that picture: Dhoni in a Manchester United jersey—not surprising, considering that's the EPL team he still supports passionately—posing with some teammates. Chhotu tells me it's from a trip to Himachal Pradesh with the Jharkhand team a few years later. Later, he shows a more recent poster of Dhoni, looking older and grizzled. 'Look at the greys. This had to happen. Being Indian captain means tension and stress, even for the coolest man on the field,' I say. But I'm immediately corrected by Chhotu. *'Nahi*, nahi. No tension for Mahi. The *safed baal* (white hair) and *daadi* (beard) is more due to all the playing in the sun. He's spent more than half his life under the sun.' Once more, I'm in no position to argue with him.

As I look around, I'm rather taken aback by the fact that Chhotu hasn't moved out of this rather ageing establishment into a more plush setting. I'm further intrigued to learn that he's not even keen on moving. 'Things have changed for sure. There's so much more competition nowadays. I've been running this right here for twenty-two years. I've stayed loyal to one brand, BAS (Beat All Sports), throughout and I don't consider myself a very ambitious person,' he explains.

It was this loyalty to BAS that helped Chhotu win the maiden sponsorship deal for his friend. Dhoni didn't play for the Royal Club for more than a season, and soon started making a name for himself in school cricket and for the CCL on the club scene. And his name started appearing routinely in the local newspapers. The friend and entrepreneur in Chhotu thought this was the right time to invest in this budding talent.

'I used to sit at BAS company back then, in Jalandhar, with Mr Kohli, the owner. I told him once, "Uncle, I have a player who is needy and doesn't even have the money to buy his own kit. Anyway, you are sponsoring two kits, just help this boy out too. Naam hai M.S. Dhoni." But he wasn't convinced. He said, "*Itni jaldi kaise hoga?* (How can this be done so quickly?)"'

But Chhotu wasn't one to give up so easily. A few days later, he was back in Mr Kohli's office with the same request. '*Bahut aage peeche, aage peeche hua* and then he kind of agreed. (After a lot of back and forth, he finally agreed.) I rushed back and told Mahi that a company is ready to sponsor him and made him prepare a CV. I went back to

Jalandhar and said, "*Paaji*, please give the kit today, he has a match in two days." He looked back and said, "Two days, na? *Chalo*, we'll see." I started shaking my head and said, "Did I say two days? I meant tomorrow,'" Chhotu says, followed by that laugh again. He returned after receiving a guarantee that the kit would be couriered soon despite multiple requests from him for it to be handed to him then and there.

The deal wasn't sealed yet. And by the time Chhotu was back in Ranchi, Dhoni had been picked in the Bihar squad for his Ranji debut. Another round of frantic calls ensued, with Chhotu screaming, 'Now his name has come in the Ranji squad. *Ab toh samaan bhej do.* (Now please send the kit.)' It was only on the eve of the match that Dhoni's first-ever kit arrived at his then home, N171, in the MECON Colony. Chhotu then points again to the picture with Dhoni in his BAS sweater.

The two had hit it off long before the BAS deal. The bike rides from the practice sessions soon got extended to Dhoni spending most of his free time at Prime Sports and playing badminton at the railway stadium once Chhotu shut shop for the day. Thus, Prime Sports became M.S. Dhoni's adda. Chhotu opened the shop around 1994 while he was still a player, and in those days, was juggling the twin roles of a cricketer and a businessman.

'This was during his CCL days. I used to close the shop by 8 p.m. We would then go and play badminton till 10 p.m., then I would drop him off at his place and head home. Around 7 a.m., I would pick him up again and drop him off for the CCL training. Around 10 to 11 a.m. he would finish practice and come to me and just sit there,' he says, pointing at the seat I'm presently occupying.

We have a customer at hand. It's a young boy, not more than fifteen, who wants a Cosco tennis ball and a pair of gloves. As they are all in the cartons and boxes next to me, I turn helper under Chhotu's instructions. I lift one here, move one there, shift myself, shift the chair, push the desk a little, and finally to Chhotu's relief, find the exact two boxes he's looking for. The transaction takes place rapidly. No questions asked. Chhotu knows exactly what size and what brand of gloves the boy needs.

'Did Mahi help while he used to sit here?' I ask rather confidently, assuming that by helping him out a little, I had provided Chhotu a Mahi throwback moment for the second time in a few hours. He looks at me funnily and replies, 'Sir, his presence was enough.' There's that Ranchi reverence again for their beloved son of the soil.

At that point, Chhotu-bhaiya starts laughing again. To my embarrassment, he's spotted that my footwear is mismatched—a slipper and a floater—which I thought I'd smartly hidden from his view.

'*Mahi ke saath rehke hum bhi sab kuch observe karna seekh gaye shayad.* (In Dhoni's company, perhaps I too have learnt to observe everything.),' he explains.

To accentuate his admiration for Dhoni's observational skills—which seem to have had a lasting impact on everyone who has met him—Chhotu gives his own version of how his friend could spot his shy father watching him bat. Amazingly, he recalls Dhoni having done so even on his Ranji debut.

'His *nazar* (eye) is all around, even when he's on the ground. I'm sure he can even spot things that happen in the crowd in the biggest stadiums in the world, and even remember a few faces. On (his Ranji) debut when he was batting (Dhoni made 40 and 68 not out in that game), his father, as usual, was peeping through one of those grooves on the boundary wall. And he spotted his father in spite of the pressure of playing his first high-level knock,' Chhotu recalls. You almost want to believe this to be true.

And according to his inner circle, it's not just a quirk. They insist that Dhoni's knack for observation makes him a great judge of people—'*aadmi turant aur achche se parakh leta hai* (he reads people quickly and correctly)', says Chhotu.

This quality of gauging a person and his credentials has come to the fore on the cricket field quite often. The Joginder Sharma example, of course, stands out, when on that famous night in Johannesburg in 2007, Dhoni handed the inexperienced medium-pacer the final over in the grand finale against Pakistan, a move that shocked the world and also eventually made India the first-ever world champions in T20 cricket. In interviews, Sharma would reveal that Dhoni not only said he would take responsibility for the decision if things went rogue but also told the young nobody that he had six balls to create history. Others around the team management would in later years emphasize that it wasn't a 'gut-feel' move but one that Dhoni had discussed earlier due to various factors—which included Sharma's ability to bowl a good yorker as well as his inherent poker face.

'He made Joginder's life. Everyone was underestimating him, but Mahi lifted him,' Chottu says and then with a smile adds, 'Your life will also change because of this book, just wait and watch.'

There have, of course, been series after series of such out-of-the-box calls that Dhoni has made in his career—many of which we'll deal with in another chapter; and while not all have been successful, they have each had the inimitable Dhoni touch. Even the times when he brought himself on to bowl that one over—like at the Champions Trophy in 2009 or before the lunch break at Lord's in 2011—just to give an unsubtle hint to the selectors about the bowling options they had given him.

It comes through even in his relationships. Chittu explains: '*Saamne se kaun aa raha hai, kyun aa raha hai, sab pata hai.* (He knows who's coming, why they're coming, everything) . . . Nobody can escape Mahi's gaze. It's the same for me as well. He'll know exactly why I have come to meet him just by looking at me. Say, I have come with a contract that needs to be signed or to introduce someone to him but I'm hesitating or talking about something else, he'll smile and say, "*Bol de, bol de. Dil mein mat rakh.* (Tell, tell, don't keep it in your heart.)"'

Now Chhotu goes on to sound like a mix of a forlorn lover and a doting parent: '*Woh din bhar mere saath hi rehta hai . . . wahan par hai, lekin mere saath hai . . . nahi lagta hai ki woh alag hai . . .* (He's always here with me . . . He may be anywhere, but he's with me . . . I don't feel that he's separate from me . . .' While Dhoni's relations with Narendra, his elder sibling, have always been a subject of conjecture—so much so that even those around him talk about it only in hushed tones and prefer not saying much even then—Chhotu had actually stood in as the bhaiya quite often in the early days. And he sounds like one even now.

'It's not like we talk to each other often. We don't have to. We're one. He has no time now, and I totally get that. But when he's in town, I'll know, and we'll certainly try and meet,' he says.

There was, of course, the famous Agartala episode in January 2001, where Dhoni was picked for the first time in the East Zone squad to play the Deodhar Trophy against South Zone. But Dhoni was blissfully unaware of his selection. It was only when Chhotu paid a routine visit to his friend, the Railways player Subra Sarkar's house the evening before the East Zone team was scheduled to fly out from Kolkata, that the news sprang upon them. Chhotu never tires of narrating the episode.

'I had just returned from one of my Jalandhar visits. BAS had launched a new wheel-wala kitbag. I went to collect it from a friend's place which was near Sarkar's house. Mahi's selection for East Zone had only appeared in the Bengali paper that Sarkar's father would get at home. As soon as I entered, his father said, "Mahi knows he's been picked to go to Agartala, right?" I said, "No, uncle, he doesn't!"' The last train to Kolkata had already left. Panic calls to the Bihar Cricket Association (BCA) and the CCL didn't yield much, and Chhotu decided to hire a Tata Sumo that very night and leave for Kolkata with Dhoni and Gautam Gupta—who would later on become Dhoni's brother-in-law after marrying his elder sister, Jayanti—for company. The car broke down during the middle of the night causing a three-hour delay, and to make matters worse, they were delayed an extra hour after being stopped by the state police for checking. That last delay meant that they couldn't make it on time for the flight. Dhoni eventually had to take a flight later in the day, which allowed Deep Dasgupta to don the gloves. Dhoni spent the match on the bench. Dasgupta managed scores of 0 and 32 not out against a power-packed South Zone attack, which included Javagal Srinath, Venkatesh Prasad and Sunil Joshi—all India regulars at that point. This was January 2001, and there are those who believe that missing the flight to Agartala delayed Dhoni's entry into international cricket by a few years, allowing Dasgupta to pip him to the post. At that stage of his career, Dhoni had appeared in nine first-class matches and had an average of 34.14. We can never say for sure how he would have fared against the likes of Srinath and Prasad at that nascent stage of his career, and the impact it would have left on him. The fact that he seemed so primed for international cricket when he did make it nearly four years later, proves that the timing of his entry too was just perfect. Maybe 2001 wasn't meant to be his time for a reason. Dasgupta did keep his place despite his failures against South Zone to face West Zone, which again had an attack comprising Ajit Agarkar and Zaheer Khan. He made scores of 2 and 0 while Dhoni watched from the sidelines—elated, as many of his friends say, to just share the same field as his idol Sachin Tendulkar.

'*Uss raat hamara banda sahi jagah pahunch nahi paaya, lekin aakhir mein sahi jagah pahunch hi gaya life mein.* (That night, our man was not able to reach the right place; but eventually, he did reach the right place in life.)' Chhotu-bhaiya couldn't have put it better.

Chhotu also recalls having experienced an epiphanic moment of Nostradamus proportions during a school league match at the Ranchi College ground. He had two friends for company, though he isn't sure whether they felt the same way he did. It wasn't a blazing knock or even one of those trademark Dhoni bludgeons that convinced Chhotu that his pillion rider was made for greatness. It was Dhoni the wicketkeeper that prompted the prediction.

'It was a catch down the leg-side he took off a fast bowler. It was a great catch, where he moved quickly and took it despite being blind-sided. *Mere dil se tabhi nikla ki yeh ek din India ke liye khelega.* (It came from my heart then that this guy would play for India one day.) My friends were taken aback. And then I remember him taking a similar catch during the last World Cup, and I was like, *yeh toh hum dekhe the aur bole bhi the* (I had seen this before, and spoken about it),' Chhotu says with a sense of great pride.

The India A tour to Kenya in 2004 is correctly identified as the tipping point for Dhoni's graduation to international cricket. This was one of the first A series to be shown live on TV back home. It couldn't have been timelier. At that point, fringe players didn't quite get the same number of A tours to show off their skills as they do now. 'A' tour performances were what you heard about and bothered to read about if you were a scrupulously keen follower of the game. And so, India got to witness Dhoni's unique repertoire of breathtaking strokes rather than just read about his two centuries in the scorecard a day later. It also helped Chhotu start a tradition of his own. He started taping all of Dhoni's exploits using a VCR on one of those 'big cassettes', as he puts it. He did it on the same small-screen TV that he still claims to keep in his shop. 'But wait, the TV is still here?' I ask.

And that sets me up for the big reveal. I picture it being part of Chhotu-bhaiya's usual routine, where he coaxes his audience into a discussion about Dhoni's India A blitzes and then springs on them the TV trick. He's still laughing as he begins moving a few cartons in front of the counter before pushing back his own tiny desk and opening a shelf, which faces inward and away from the road, making it completely hidden from view. I wonder whether it always requires such elaborate shifting or it's just part of the show. The drama is totally worth it. He even has to move some of the apparel—a few T-shirts and a couple of shorts—for the 12-inch TV to be finally revealed. So clandestine is the location that Q of James Bond fame might be proud of it.

'I don't like going to the ground to watch games. I prefer it right here on this old TV. But I always watch it on mute. And because of its location, nobody outside can ever make out I'm watching TV and that too a cricket match,' he says.

Chhotu remembers having asked Dhoni for two gifts from Kenya—two centuries, preferably against Pakistan, which is exactly what his friend got him. In return, Chhotu played the perfect elder sibling, recording the entire innings and then taking TV grabs and sticking them up for display all around his enterprise.

While describing some of Dhoni's shots from those knocks, Chhotu gets up and cleans the photos with a cloth and a lot of care. It's something that he has to do often, considering the proximity to the bustling and dusty Sujata Chowk. He also has thousands of newspaper clippings dating back from 1995–96. 'You're the real Dhoni chronicler,' I tell him. Chhotu smiles.

Dhoni had crossed single figures only once in his first three ODI innings. So, when India met Pakistan in the second ODI in Vizag on 5 April 2005, India's new wicketkeeper had a lot to prove. Dhoni had batted at No. 7 in all those previous innings. That morning, Chhotu paid a visit to his gurudwara.

'I prayed, "*Babaji, aaj iska test hai.* (Babaji, today he has a test.)" If Mahi comes up the order today, he'll make it count. When Chottu came back to the shop and switched on his trusted TV, Sachin Tendulkar was walking back, run out for just 2. And in walked Dhoni. His first scoring shot was a punch-drive on the up off Mohammad Sami that went between bowler and mid-off for four. It's an area of the ground where he rarely scores. But it was a shot that had both oomph and a touch of arrogance.

'I saw that boundary and thought, today he'll score a century. His career hasn't looked back since that boundary,' recalls Chhotu about the 123-ball 148 that set the Dhoni career off with a bang.

It only got better a day later as Dhoni returned to great fanfare in his home town and celebrated what would be the first of many epoch-defining feats with his core group of Chittu, Chhotu and Gautam-da over dinner at their favourite dhaba. Yes, the 'dhabhe mein khane wala' had made it big but not forgotten his roots.

Chhotu and Greg Chappell share something in common. They both predicted that Dhoni would become Indian captain long before anyone even imagined him as a candidate or even thought of it as a probability. While Chappell would famously declare this during a selection meeting, Chhotu would shock those around him with the same claim. But somehow, and here's where the protectiveness of being a bhaiya kicks in, Chhotu says he was suspicious of the motives behind naming Dhoni as the Indian captain for the inaugural World T20. This is a common thread you see with the Ranchi folk, a prevailing sense of suspicion over a lot of decisions taken around their friend and idol. It's perhaps a small-town thing, this near-paranoia, but in Dhoni's context, their distrust is just another extension of their genuine concern for him.

'A lot of people were after him. They made him captain within two years for a reason. There's a conspiracy behind it, we thought then. T20 was considered a random format back then, and they thought, make him captain, he won't do well and we can get rid of him from the team itself,' Chhotu spells out the conspiracy. Not that it affected his confidence about Dhoni overcoming even this unlikely challenge.

'I knew he would do well and win the World T20. Those who dig a hole for others, fall into it themselves.

That fact will always remain—he has never done bad things to anyone. He kept doing his thing and continued to give it his best, even today,' he adds.

The World T20 victory changed Dhoni's profile around India, and especially in Ranchi. He could no longer make visits to Prime Sports without the entire road being cordoned off. And with time, he and Chhotu-bhaiya began to drift apart, only physically though, as I'm told repeatedly.

Chhotu recalls having given a young Dhoni only one piece of cricketing advice. 'Stay at the crease, and the runs will always come to you.' I bring up the subject of the elder-brother role that he has been playing in Dhoni's life, and Chhotu sheepishly tells me, 'By the time I could give him any life advice: he'd grown too big for me, in stature anyway.' The common perception about Dhoni in many circles is that he doesn't let anyone get too close to him. Chhotu disagrees. 'Whoever is with him, is with him for life.'

Funnily enough, these days Dhoni plays bhaiya to Chhotu's eleven-year-old son, Simar Singh. But before we get to that, I am shown a video of young Simar batting on a local ground. 'The feet are moving well,' I observe. Pat comes the reply from the father: '*Haath nahi theek aa raha hai.* (The hands are not moving correctly.) It's been four months now.'

When the Singhs do visit the Dhoni household, cricket, as always, is off the menu. Simar though is allowed a few indulgences.

'He goes there and plays cards with Mahi and his wife,' Chhotu says. '*Badi kum umar mein sikha diya hai aapne usse?*

(Haven't you taught him to play cards at too young an age?),' I say, and he replies, 'Sir, he's not only learnt it on his own, he's also taught Mahi and Sakshi those card games.'

Cricket rarely features in conversations involving Chittu, Chhotu and Mahi. That's been the case right from the school days, both his closest confidants admit. There are enough common interests otherwise to keep them distracted from bats and balls. I am repeatedly subjected to one of them during my visit to Prime Sports. As we are talking, Chhotu-bhaiya has sent his apprentice on a number of occasions to get chai. At times, the tea is accompanied by biscuits and pastries.

'Whenever the three of us are together, there'll be lots of chai and lots of comedy. Before he became a star, we never talked cricket. Now he's a superstar and we still don't talk cricket. *Woh khel raha hai, aur hum hamara kaam kar rahe hai.* (He's playing, and we are doing our own thing.) It's a simple equation,' says Chhotu. He too then brings up the McDowell's No. 1 Soda ad featuring him and Chittu, though not as gushingly as his partner-in-crime, and mentions the chai scene in it. This is about Dhoni complaining about Chittu's sugarless tea, and how he himself makes the best chai among all the three.

This has been a running gag among them for years now. Chittu had insisted that Dhoni's simplicity came through in the ad too while he speaks about sipping 'Chittu's *kharaab* (bad) chai'. 'Even when you give him a cup of tea, if there's slightly less sugar, he'll drink it, but once he's done, he'll say, "*Thodi cheeni kum tha. Pehle nahi bolega, last mein bolega.*

(The sugar was less. He won't say it at first, but only at the end.),'" Chittu had said.

Like with Chittu, Chhotu-bhaiya too understands his role very clearly in the Dhoni journey, and how it's changed with time despite their relationship remaining the same. This is the main reason they've managed to stay so close to this complex enigma in a simple avatar. And one of Dhoni's characteristics they both harp on is that he never forgets those who have helped him.

'But at the same time, we never expected anything in return. We realized that we were just playing our roles in this special journey. None of us who have remained close to him did it with any other intention. It was always unconditional. All I did was introduce him to BAS. They helped him. *Yeh aage pahunch gaya. Company ka bhi achcha ho gaya. MS ka bhi achcha ho gaya. Aur hamara bhi achcha ho gaya.* (He went ahead. The company benefitted. MS benefitted. And we too benefitted.),' Chhotu quips.

He then thinks back to those multiple bike rides, and sums up like everyone who's been part of the whole Dhoni journey does, that the man has overall remained the same. Chhotu recalls how you could never make out whether he had had a good day or a bad one based on his demeanour.

'He would just be there sitting quietly. On and off, he would say something, but his focus was always only on his game.' It's this incredible and distinctive equanimity of his friend that Chhotu believes will keep their friendship going the same way it always has.

'*Woh run maare, tabh mere saath hoga, jab nahi maarega, tabhi bhi mere saa. i hoga.* (If he scores runs, he's with us; if he doesn't, he's still with us.) It was the same in his schooldays. *Tabhi bhi mera dost tha, aaj India ke liye khel raha hain, abhi bhi mera dost hai.* (Then too he was my friend, and now that he's playing for India, he still remains my friend.)'

Dhoni's love for Ranchi is one reason Chhotu is confident—no, this is not one of his predictions—that it'll be like the old days all over again once his playing days are over. 'I don't think he'll ever leave Ranchi and go. Finally, he'll have time for us again once he decides to retire. That part will never change. *Mahal mein rehna bhi pata hai, aur chote se kamre mein bhi. Jab nahi tha, waise hi tha. Jab bahut hai, waisa hi hai* . . . (He knows how to live in a palace and also in a small room. When he didn't have anything, he was like that. Now when he has a lot, he's still like that . . .) That's Mahi.'

5

The *Fauji* Captain

On the morning of 17 March 2017, the Jharkhand one-day team had to hastily evacuate ITC Welcome, a five-star hotel in Delhi's Dwarka area. The players were having breakfast when they suddenly encountered thick smoke emanating from a fire that had broken out in one part of the property. There was understandable panic in the restaurant area. But one member of the Jharkhand team that was in Delhi for the Vijay Hazare Trophy (fifty-over domestic tournament) was in a strange way feeling exhilarated.

It was he who took charge of the evacuation procedure, coolly and calmly asking his teammates to not go hunting for their mobile phones and instead, assemble at a particular spot before getting out safely. This wasn't M.S. Dhoni in his Captain Cool avatar. This was honorary Lt Col Mahendra Singh Dhoni from the 106 Parachute Regiment of the Territorial Army leading his troops towards safety in a perilous mission.

Thankfully, the Jharkhand team escaped unscathed but their match had to be postponed since their kitbags were stuck inside the hotel.

A few days later, Dhoni would recount the incident with great excitement to Colonel Vembu Shankar, his close army associate and dear friend. The hotel fire was, after all, exactly the kind of crisis scenario that the two would often discuss dealing with. In these discussions, they often imagined Dhoni making a quick escape through kitchens and secret doors to avoid the mob eagerly awaiting an opportunity to catch a glimpse of him in every hotel lobby around the country, and at times, even overseas. As Col Shankar reveals, there would be a very obvious spring in his friend's stride as they would reach Dhoni's car parked in an undisclosed section of the hotel through a dark alley. In these brief yet thrilling moments, he would get to play the one role that he's most desperately wanted to in life—and one that's unlikely to ever come his way: M.S. Dhoni the fauji.

'Most of his exit routes would involve some part of the basement with no phone signal, and even as we would be guided out by one of the hotel staff, he would ask, "*Abhi kuch ho gaya toh, kaise niklenge?* (If something happens now, how will we escape?)" His mind is always working at how we can improvise and react to emergency situations. He was quite thrilled about having taken charge during that Delhi fire incident,' Col Shankar says.

The colonel, himself a gallantry award winner who has now retired, isn't the only Dhoni confidant who insists that '*woh dil, deemag se pura fauji hai* (he's a complete soldier, in heart and mind)'. Col Shankar goes on to say that if he'd been in the army, Dhoni would have made a great leader, even if he didn't rise to being a general or a brigadier, because, as he explains, 'MS is not too great at long-distance running and I'm not sure if he would have had an interest in the studies needed to finish courses and rise through the ranks.' But Col Shankar is confident that Dhoni would have led good and successful operations, and been a great leader to those serving under him. He points to the Delhi fire incident again as an example.

'Such thinking at a juncture of adversity is what a leader should be able to do. I can suggest lovely ideas while speaking, but if I don't do anything when there is such a thing as a fire, then I'm not a leader.' He also believes what makes M.S. Dhoni probably the best fauji that isn't to be is how he understands the core of the army and the pulse of the soldiers. '"The core of the army is the soldiers, how they live, how they train and how they fight. He understands it the best.'

There's perhaps a link there somewhere between Dhoni the hypothetical military leader and Dhoni the former cricket captain of India. He was neither the most successful player in the team—at the point when he took over—nor the most distinguished, another traditional expectation from an Indian captain, and didn't hail from one of the major cricket centres of the country either. He was if anything the first small-town superstar to take over the most coveted job in Indian team sport. His decisions were not always popular and often perplexing, but everyone watching knew they were taken with the kind of conviction that you see on the frontline.

Most importantly, there are very few who played under him who don't vouch for his leadership skills as he led them through many a successful operation. He was in many ways, India's first and only fauji captain.

But Dhoni didn't have any soldier friends while growing up. Even Chittu is bemused at just when or how his longest-standing friend developed this love and obeisance for the armed forces. He doesn't even remember him talking much about the military or the army, which is not surprising considering he doesn't usually say much. In his meetings with Dhoni though, Col Shankar came to know that Dhoni had an innate desire to join the army, a childhood obsession even. Though circumstances didn't quite allow him to pursue his dream, the drive remained as strong as ever.

As his cricket career advanced, Dhoni was lucky enough to experience a few brushes with the military and even a few of their establishments like the National Defence Academy (NDA) and the Indian Military Academy (IMA)—places he could only dream of visiting as a young man. The NDA visit was with the Indian team in the mid-2000s and he'd visited the IMA with a friend. Then came his first encounter with the Parachute Regiment in 2006, when the then Indian coach Greg Chappell decided to take the Rahul Dravid-led team to its training centre in Bangalore. It wasn't simply a feel-good exercise though, as the Indian players were put through the grind, and had to undertake activities ranging from shooting, rock climbing, grenade throwing and many obstacle courses. By all accounts, Dhoni topped all the obstacle courses and proved to be even better than some of the jawans. The video-game buff also got a taste of simulation exercises like infiltrating enemy territory and rescuing hostages. Dhoni also learnt a trait during that five-hour visit, which would in years to come make him the most popular non-army visitor at every military camp across the country. He has learnt to talk in the jawan tongue.

'Being a Hindi-speaking guy, he could easily relate to the jawans more than anyone else. Typically, he would always find a fellow Ranchi guy and he would say, "*Aap mere gaon ke ho.* (You are from my village.)" Things like that. People would also come to him and say the same,' says Col Shankar.

According to the colonel though, the tipping point in Dhoni's enduring love affair with the military came when he paid the National Security Guard (NSG) commandos a visit in Manesar on Republic Day 2009. It was part of an NDTV programme, and Dhoni could be seen in commando gear, overcoming his fear of heights by successfully completing a rock-climbing drill. But not before a quip to his trainer about needing an external boost to calm his nerve.

Later in the show, he delivered an emotional ode to the NSG for their efforts in the terror siege of 2008 in Mumbai: 'When the attack started and I watched it on TV, my first thought was, "Where is the NSG?" I knew that once you guys step in, the victory would be ours. What you did was remarkable and I thank you for it.' There, he also showcases his dry humour while narrating a Rajinikanth joke to the commandos as well as while clamping down on their queries about the then bachelor's marital plans. On the latter, he said, '*Udte huye panchi key par kyon kaatna chahtey ho?* (Why are you trying to clip the wings of an air-borne bird?)'

Dhoni also got to meet a lot of other army officers in addition to the NSG commandos during his full-day visit and became great friends with a few of them—some still remain a part of his fauji circle.

Dhoni, Col Shankar says, then wanted a taste of the actual stuff by getting a feel of where the jawans lived and the sacrifices they make at the border. 'What we get to see in Colaba (Navy Nagar and a few other military colonies), for example, is the peacetime army. He wanted to know the army from the bottom-up and not by looking at it from a general's view,' he says.

One of his friends from the NDTV-NSG visit to Manesar took Dhoni around Manesar and even got him to experience one of the most challenging and testing posts in the army. And Dhoni perhaps became the first Indian cricketer to take his position at a sentry post, even if it was for a brief while. 'He wanted to see how a sentry feels at night. In the night, everything seems to be moving. Even static objects seem to be moving. That's how the night is. He actually wanted to know how people react at that sentry post. Because, a sentry is guarding so many people. Even if you're a sepoy with just two years of service, you can't be waiting for any general's orders to fire,' Col Shankar explains.

And standing at sentry posts is also what young trainee officers are made to undergo.

'Just how he knew it was the right thing to do without any formal training like us boggles my mind,' he says. I hear a lot of declarations of astonishment from Colonel Shankar during our chat. Dhoni came out of the NSG visit more determined than ever to form some sort of association with his real passion.

'He mentions that visit many, many times. He'll keep referring back to running into some of the soldiers he had met there. He's met thousands of faujis in the years after that, but he keeps mentioning those guys in particular, and has stayed in touch with them after nearly a decade. The boot camp in 2006 gave him the feeling that "if I were in the army, I would have done well". But it was with the NSG that he was properly exposed to training and weapons, and made fauji friends,' Col Shankar says.

To be one of his fauji friends comes with certain concessions and even greater privileges. It means you're often on a higher pedestal than anyone else, including Amitabh Bachchan.

His phone might remain unreachable regardless of who you are, but he's the most active member of the WhatsApp group that he shares with his fauji friends. He might fail to pick up Bachchan's phone call on his birthday but he never fails to call Manoj-bhaiya—a former military man turned security head at the Jharkhand State Cricket

Association (JSCA) stadium in Ranchi and whose special chai Dhoni considers his true poison—and wish his family every new year. Dhoni's almost strange apathy towards his phone is legendary, so is the list of people who have been on the receiving end of the Dhoni no-show on the phone.

And try as he might, Col Shankar struggles to mask the envy in his voice when he talks about the activity on MS's fauji WhatsApp group which he shares with his closest army friends. On that group, Dhoni, who's the last person to use his phone as a social-media tool, shares pictures of himself and discusses the goings-on in his life, which even the colonel isn't always privy to.

Dhoni doesn't like alcohol. He's rather vocal about his aversion to it. Some close to him say it's the smell that bothers him—especially that of champagne and beer. To the extent that he is known to change his room even if there's a whiff of it around. You won't find him in the dressing room if the team is celebrating a win by spraying champagne around, like after the Johannesburg Test win in 2006 when the Indian players went a little berserk. It was, after all, their first-ever Test win in South Africa. And it was only the fourteenth Test of Dhoni's career, but he preferred to wait outside on the grassy bank right outside the dressing room at the Bullring and held his ground even as some of his teammates exuberantly ran around him carrying the bubbly and drenching each other with beer and orange juice. The wild celebration even prompted the then coach Greg Chappell to hold forth on 'drinking rather than pouring' beer.

Dhoni himself has often said it's the 'bitter taste' of liquor that puts him off from drinking it. But he also has never had an issue with others around him indulging in it. Those in Ranchi recall how in his younger days he would make it a point to ensure that his closest friends always had a nice time while celebrating one of his cricketing achievements, and he would sit in the middle with a glass of drink which he rarely sipped out of even as others guzzled away.

But this pales in comparison when he plays the overindulgent host whenever his fauji friends visit him. According to someone very close to him, that's the only time even Dhoni has a drink. Not according to Col Shankar, though. It's again more a case of him being a gracious host and ensuring that the guests have the best time possible and that they are at complete ease.

Dhoni doesn't appreciate cigarettes either. But in his younger days, he would often buy cigarettes from duty-free shops while on foreign tours for one of his closest friends. However, he wouldn't hand them over without a taunt: 'Mere paise se tu kudhki zindagi jala raha hai. (You are sending your life up in smoke on my dime.)'

Such concessions also extend to that prickly affair that annoys not just cricketers but also cricket journalists—the demand for match tickets. I can't tell you how many relatives and friends I have fallen out with just because I've not been able to provide what they assume I owe them. 'What's the point of you being a cricket reporter if you can't get your cousin sister a couple of IPL tickets?' How I've tired of listening to this rant year after year even as my honest pleas of 'Wait, I just get an accreditation to cover the bloody thing. Why would anyone give me tickets?' would fall on deaf, stubborn ears. At least, Dhoni has the excuse of never answering his phone, not to mention that he's slightly less accessible than I am.

On IPL match days, the fauji group goes into overdrive, with demands that far outstrip the reasonable. 'Players generally get four tickets, and as captain, MS would get an extra couple. It's easier for home matches but it's for the away matches that you have to oblige the teammates from the host city. His phone would be flooded with messages saying "minimum I need 4 tickets" or "*jyaada nahi* (not a lot), 7 tickets needed",' says Col Shankar, while revealing that he has seen Dhoni going out of his way and even managing twelve to fifteen tickets if one of his army buddies asked for them. In one instance, one of his fauji friends got shocked by just how far his cricketer friend could go. 'One of them had messaged him for seven tickets, and a few days later, MS told me, "*Arrey*, he never came to collect them." When I informed the *fauji* concerned, he just couldn't believe Dhoni had actually taken the effort to make it happen.'

Dhoni doesn't usually give tickets to anyone else who contacts him directly. His rationale is that if the person is big enough to reach him, then he certainly must have access to a politician or a high-ranking government official to get the tickets. 'They must have already done jugaad. MS is just a backup and also they can flaunt that Dhoni gave them a ticket. MS knows this all too well,' Col Shankar explains.

On most other occasions, it's the housekeeping staff or the waiters in the restaurants who end up as the beneficiaries. It's rather common for the last guy who cleans Dhoni's room to be asked whether anyone at home would want to watch that night's match, or for a waiter on the morning shift to receive a call from the restaurant with a simple message: 'I've kept two tickets for you at the front desk.'

What Dhoni appreciates the most about his military friends is the way they treat him. They take liberties with him; Col Shankar says they 'treat him like a commando buddy, with mock disdain, like he's just one of the boys'. They tell him that he's just some lowly cricketer and is no match for their real heroes. Dhoni loves such banter since at some deep level, he likes being treated like a regular guy. It's a break from the hero worship that is doled out everywhere else. They criticize him too, mostly to get under his skin, and generally about the nitty-gritties of his beloved uniform, the one he received while being commissioned as an honorary lieutenant colonel.

'They'll say he's wearing it wrong or that his dress is crumpled,' says Col Shankar. But, for someone who's dealt with criticism and public scrutiny for years, these tongue-in-cheek barbs really rattle Dhoni. So much so that he would come to the colonel, and like an adolescent who's been picked on at school, say, '*Usne aisa bata diya, sir. Aapne bataya nahi ki aise lagana hai isse.* (He made fun of me, sir. But you never told me that this was how it should be worn.)'

When MS Dhoni was conferred with the rank of honorary lieutenant colonel in the Territorial Army of India on 1 November 2011, he didn't take off his uniform the whole day. The ceremony took place at around 9 a.m. in Delhi, there was a press conference at 4.30 p.m., and it was only at around 11 p.m. that the then Indian captain could bear to temporarily part with his treasured 'olive greens'.

'Everything else you can buy. But you can't buy a uniform. That's something you earn. He was very happy about it. That gave him a lot of confidence,' says Col Shankar.

The ceremony was attended only by Sakshi and the major from the NSG—incognito—whom Dhoni by then had grown very close to. Col Shankar would meet him later that evening and find his friend beaming like he'd never seen him beam before. They had met for the first time at a dinner organized by Col Shankar's friend in the midst of India's Test against South Africa in Kolkata in February 2010.

The colonel is an autograph collector and is obsessed with his sporting idols, 'especially those who captured our imaginations in that period between 1983 and 1991', ranging from Patrick Patterson to Sergey Bubka. Once, the colonel was in Mumbai to get an autograph from Bubka on a couple of caricatures. The pole vault legend was there as the chief ambassador of the Mumbai Marathon, and Col Shankar had travelled all the way just to catch Bubka for a couple of minutes. For such a fanboy, it came as unbelievable news—some eight years ago—to know that Dhoni would be having dinner with him.

'There were some four–five of us, and I couldn't believe that the Indian captain would come for dinner in the middle of a Test. No cricket was spoken about. I took a few autographs. It was his knowledge about the air force and army weapons which intrigued me. For someone rumoured to never read newspapers or watch TV, he had in-depth information about what items the army was procuring and what was in the arsenal of some other countries. He was inquisitive too. What also stood out for me was how he looked at the army. No jingoism on the lines of "our soldiers are sacrificing their lives", but very, very practical,' Col Shankar recounts his first meeting with Dhoni.

Shankar would soon take Dhoni along to various military establishments around the country but there would be a lot of protocol to be followed. Around a year later, they began discussing how to get the new World Cup–winning captain officially associated with the army so that, among other things, he could visit even more military establishments. Col Shankar and a few of his colleagues approached the then army chief General V.K. Singh with a proposal. Kapil Dev, the last man to have lifted the World Cup trophy, and the legendary Malayalam actor Mohan Lal had already been made honorary lieutenant colonels. But it wasn't smooth sailing, for the air force too wanted Dhoni on their ranks. Wing Commander M. Baladitya, who'd been team India's manager for a number of years, was the keenest proponent. He'd already roped in Sachin Tendulkar as a group captain. In fact, just three days after Dhoni hit Nuwan Kulasekara for that famous six in the direction of the hockey stadium adjacent to Wankhede, Wg Cdr Baladitya was at the then air force chief P.V. Naik's residence, and plans were being made for Dhoni to fly in an Su-30MKI.

Dhoni, though, was to remain loyal to his childhood fixation with the army. He had only one request: to be allowed to join the Parachute Regiment. His decision did take Col Shankar slightly by surprise. 'He had called Ranchi home for most of his life and could have joined the Bihar Regiment. He then had this special adopted home link with Chennai and could have joined the Madras Regiment,' he says. But Dhoni, like always, had a valid explanation for his choice.

'He wanted to join the Parachute Regiment. Number one, because it's a volunteer force. Number two is that it's pan-India. So, they are not people from one particular state or region. That intrigued him,' explains Col Shankar.

There were other perks as well. Being a paratrooper is considered elite. So, Dhoni knew that they would have more exciting missions than the regular army. Moreover, most of his friends from the NSG were paratroopers. Col Shankar recalls that the army was slightly apprehensive as it didn't want Dhoni to be a figurehead like other celebrity inductees who would just come for an odd event here or there, and maybe even charge money for coming. Finally, they decided to dovetail Dhoni's conferment ceremony with Olympic medal–winner Abhinav Bindra's who too became an honorary lieutenant colonel that day.

For all his excitement regarding the rank, Dhoni was most excited to be in the olive green uniform. This was his childhood dream coming alive. And so obsessed is he with it that he carries a set everywhere he goes, much to

Col Shankar's bewilderment. 'I'll say, "No chance you'll get to wear it, especially during an IPL match. You'll come this afternoon, practise and go for the match. Next morning, you have to leave." "*Nahi,* sir, *kaheen mil gaya toh chance* (No, sir, what if I get a chance), and I end up going there in a T-shirt and jeans." I've realized that more than anything, it's that uniform that fascinates him the most,' says Shankar, who isn't at all surprised to have seen Dhoni proudly donning his uniform and marching towards the podium to receive his Padma Bhushan award in April 2018.

Now an official member of the army, Dhoni has started visiting even more army establishments, including a visit to the Hindustan Aeronautics Limited (HAL) factory where he got introduced to even newer weapons.

With his Test retirement in late 2014 freeing him up, Dhoni decided it was time to earn a badge and add more glory to his already glorious uniform, which at that point simply carried a Territorial Army logo, the paratroopers sign and his rank on the shoulder with the name tag above the right breast pocket. The uniform, as he would tell Col Shankar, was looking '*sukha, sukha*' (dry).

The honorary lieutenant colonel now wanted a 'para wing' added to it, and a badge with blue wings and an umbrella, for which he would have to complete five parachute jumps at the end of a rigorous fourteen–fifteen-day training schedule. After getting permission from the Board of Control for Cricket in India (BCCI) and clearance from the defence ministry, Dhoni reported at the 50th Parachute Brigade in Agra. There he would stay in the barracks, wake up at 4 a.m. like everyone else and go through the rigours for the whole day at the Para Training Centre. But while the rest of the jawans would get to rest and recuperate after the physically draining day, the celebrity trainee had to contend with various social commitments, from drinking chai with the superiors to inaugurating an event. In fourteen days, he visited thirty different places, including one government school—he later said that none of the kids knew who he was.

At the end of the rigorous training session, it was time for the jump. His first jump came off an An-32 military aircraft from around 15,000 feet. But as he would tell Col Shankar later, it was the second that was the toughest. "'*First jump mein pata nahi chalta hai*. (The first jump you don't realize what's happening.) I was just pushed out. Only then you realize, bloody how crazy this is. The second jump is the toughest. You know what's going to happen, and you're waiting, waiting,'" Shankar recalls him saying. 'You are in a fixed line and just pushed out. It is generally safe since the parachute opens on its own, you don't have to do anything,' he explains.

Completing the five jumps and earning his badge also meant forming a stronger bond with the regiment he represented. Moreover, the fact that not many of his fauji friends, Col Shankar included, had completed the five jumps, gave his feat an additional shine. "'*Sir, aapne toh nahi kiya hai*. (Sir, you have not done it.),'" Col Shankar recalls Dhoni telling him soon after with great glee.

That wasn't the only time Dhoni indulged in one-upmanship with the colonel. He does so every time the two go to a shooting range. Whenever possible, Dhoni makes sure that he visits one on 1 January, regardless of which part of the world he's in. The shooting range is his *kolaideivyam* (Tamil for family deity), says Col Shankar, who remembers picking him up at 6 a.m. from Taj Bengal on New Year's Day a few years ago. And also seeing him up and ready, decked up immaculately in his uniform.

Col Shankar says that Dhoni can fire any weapon—he's seen the former Indian captain do it with at least nine different weapons—from twenty-five yards and hit the bullseye. It's something you expect only the most highly skilled soldier to pull off. The fact that he can do so even with a pistol, which jumps a lot more on recoil, impresses Col Shankar so much that he reiterates the point.

'Any firing is about holding, aiming and the trigger operation. Nobody has taught him the basics, but they seem ingrained in him. His strength is amazing, so the grip is great. The aiming comes from the natural alignment of his body and, of course, he's worked hard to master the technique of trigger operation. Normally, we soldiers pick a new weapon and spend the first round only on zeroing. He picks up, and within two shots, he has gained enough information about the weapon to strike bull,' he explains.

The irrepressible competitor in Dhoni naturally makes sure that every visit to the shooting range results in a 'shoot-out' between the two friends. 'He beats me hollow every time and will even tease me saying things like, "*Sir, aap hamesha daaye–baaye maarte ho.* (Sir, you always strike right or left of the target." I always tell him that in combat I've proved myself and killed terrorists. "You've only proved yourself on the range." That's our standard banter. But you can see how thrilled he is to get the better of an active soldier,' Col Shankar says with a beaming smile. He also quickly recalls the time Dhoni beat former Australian pace great Glenn McGrath, a lifelong hunter, at a clay-pigeon shooting face-off in Kimberley during the 2009 IPL which was played in South Africa. And he did so as clinically and cerebrally as he finishes off a run chase.

Dhoni takes his ravenous curiosity to the shooting range too, and as Col Shankar says, he won't just pick up a new weapon and fire away. It's not just some trigger-happy indulgence for him. Instead, he'll go into the mechanics of it, ask why it's particularly better than others, or he'll read up on them and give seasoned officers information that they wouldn't have been aware of, like 'Sir, there are certain weapons that'll give you sight where the laser pointer is and very few Indian weapons have that.' He'll also want to know whether the one he's hitting 'bull' with will be as effective in combat as it is on the range. 'It's again something we are taught as young officers—to first understand a weapon in its entirety before learning to fire it,' says Col Shankar.

In an army establishment, it's a different Dhoni that shows up. When the colonel and Dhoni are together in his room or on the road—when he often picks on the cricket-mad colonel, saying, '*Sir, aap IPL mein kya*

kar rahe ho? Doklam mein hona chahiye aapko. (Sir, what are you doing in IPL? You should be in Doklam.)' But when they visit a military unit, he makes it a point to play second fiddle to the colonel. He acknowledges the hierarchy and respects it.

'He salutes really well now,' says the colonel. 'Now he doesn't get confused with ranks. It's easy for a civilian to get confused with military jargon. Prior to such visits, he'll ask me, "*Isko kaise bulana hai? Kaunse regiment ka hai? Bahut log aa gaye toh kaise bulana hai.* (How should I address him? Which regiment is he from? When a lot of people come, how do I address them?) Who should be the priority?"' says Col Shankar. And Dhoni doesn't mind erring on the side of overdoing the respect, even if it means addressing every fauji he meets at a camp as 'sir'.

It's at these army bases that Dhoni's 'innate knowledge' about military life really shines through, leaving Col Shankar flabbergasted every time. While celebrity visits are largely publicized, Dhoni insists on informing the people incharge only at the last minute. That's not to keep them guessing but to ensure that his audience isn't restricted to the best people they have or simply officers with their wives. Dhoni always prefers meeting the jawans since he feels he can make a bigger difference to their lives, and also because he connects with them more in terms of background, work ethic and an earthy approach to life.

Col Shankar would call beforehand and ask for thirty–forty jawans to be quickly assembled, and the initial volley of questions to Dhoni would all involve cricket, along with a few about his personal life, especially after the movie came out. But Dhoni, of course, as any journalist who has attended even a single press conference of his would know, has this ability to effortlessly steer a question you want answered towards one that he wants to answer. As Col Shankar says, he does it subtly without sounding rude and manages to tug at the jawans' heartstrings.

As Col Shankar reveals, he would start telling them about how his father wasn't a big shot and that, much like them, he's away from his home and family for long periods. He once told a bunch of them that at his peak, he got forty days off in a year, out of which he had brand endorsements to deal with, leaving him with not more than eight to nine days in a year at home.

'He tells them, "I am exactly like you. But at least you guys have the freedom to go meet your friends and relatives on your off days. I am mainly cocooned in my hotel, and it's almost like a jail to me." He also slips in lines such as, like them he too has to take care of his finances despite all his wealth, which immediately strikes a chord with the jawans,' Col Shankar says.

Soon, it's Dhoni who's asking questions, mainly centred around the agricultural land that invariably an average jawan owns or tends to back home. They'll range from who's taking care of them to how the crop is this time. That again makes the soldiers' eyes light up, says the colonel. "They'll start telling him stories excitedly. "*Saheb, iss baar baarish*

hi nahi hui. Papa ne aisa kiya. Beej mein humne yeh daala.
(Saheb, this time there was no rains. Papa tried to do this.
In between, we tried to sow this.)'"

In the army, young officers are made to live with
the jawans. It's part of their grooming process, paving
the making of a good military leader. The stay can last
anywhere between two weeks to two months, depending
on the regiment. Col Shankar reveals that in some Gorkha
units, the officer cannot enter the officer's mess for food till
he's learnt to speak Nepali fluently. 'The guys in the unit
there speak only Nepali. So, they make sure you know the
language properly. If you are from a Muslim unit, you have
to go for prayers to know what namaz is about. It's done so
that we can lead them effortlessly,' he says.

Having a drink with a jawan or going to the *bara khana*
(a feast organized on special occasions) even if the food is
saltier than what your dietary demands dictate, rather than
sticking to the mess is a great way of bonding. It's a tradition
that is passed down generation after generation of senior
officers to their successors.

Dhoni, of course, has had no formal training in becoming
an officer or a military leader. But heck, he's barely had
formal training to be a cricketer. He just found his own way
of becoming one. But like Col Shankar keeps reiterating,
Dhoni just seems to have an inherent understanding of
the significance of bonding with the soldiers. Or like he
says with the same astonishment as always, 'Where did he
get that from?' For, while Dhoni is known to rarely have
anything more than a piece of chicken or a glass of water
when presented with a gourmet feast at the officer's mess,

he doesn't miss out on a single item offered to him from the soldiers' kitchen.

'He'll relish the jawans' chai handed to him in a steel glass. He'll barely touch the continental and English fare laid out by the officers, but with the jawans he'll have one small piece of the pakora and taste all the sweets. He realizes that it makes a difference to their lives. They'll say, "*Dhoni saheb ne yeh khaya.* (Dhoni saheb ate this.)" They'll talk about it forever,' says Col Shankar.

The colonel further explains that there's no greater satisfaction for an officer when a soldier who served under him comes to him after many years and says, '*Yaad hai mein aapke saath wahan tha? Aap bahut achche the.* (Remember, I was there with you? You were very good.)' That's exactly the feedback Col Shankar gets from those who have interacted with Dhoni. 'They'll say, "*Dhoni saheb kya achcha bole the. Maine bhi ghar mein jaake bataya.* (How well Dhoni sir spoke. I told my family too.)" The same jawan will then say that while MS wanted only group photos, they managed to sneak in a selfie with him.'

It's often how happy the soldiers are under an officer's command that determines his annual appraisal. The jawans might not be the one writing the final report, but the man who is, does so only after taking their opinion. It can be little things like whether you sacrificed watching a movie to attend one of their unit events.

'We also have the usual yardsticks ranging up to "outstanding". But if your boss writes that you are a good asset both in war and peace, then you have achieved the highest honour,' says Col Shankar. Like Dhoni did when former

India coach Gary Kirsten said, 'I want to go to war with this guy,' a few months after the two had seen India lift the World Cup on that famous night at the Wankhede stadium.

Most of Dhoni's conversations at these army camps— and he's now visited a lot of them, from the southern part of the country to Kashmir and Leh in the very north—are bond-building exercises with the jawans. He also tells them how they idolize him while he looks up to them.

As captain, Dhoni has earned many sobriquets—from that of being an impulsive gambler, an astute tactician, to a rather reactionary sceptic in Test cricket. But he has never ever shied away from taking a decision on his own terms, whether it made sense or not to the outside world or even his teammates. And decision-making is an issue that he gets quizzed on a lot by the soldiers he meets by the dozens. He, however, uses it as a platform to declare his views on how war and cricket should never be spoken of in the same breath, forget putting on the same pedestal.

'He tells them "the more and more decisions you take, the more and more times you'll make a correct decision. So the more decisions you take, the number of mistakes will come down." He says in war, it is life and death. You might not get another chance. When people say India–Pakistan match *ek jung hai* (is war), he says that's completely wrong. People lose lives and there's destruction. Not only of the army but the whole country,' says Col Shankar.

Dhoni is also aware of the ills of the army, whether it is to do with the bureaucracy or the lack of equipment, and he questions them wherever he goes. He's found that if the right people are asked the tough questions, they sit up and realize that they cannot fake it with him. A young Dhoni is said to have been similar in the Indian dressing room, at that point boasting of some of the biggest names in the history of the sport. He never spoke out of line, but he never shied away from making his point of view heard either. If he had a point, he would make it.

It was a trait that he displayed a lot as Indian captain. He remained steadfast in calling a spade a spade or in pointing out the white elephant in the room even if there were times in his career when critics said that he could have done more of it.

When he led India for the first time during the triangular series in Australia back in 2007–08, Dhoni was clear about not wanting a particular senior batsman in the lineup. He had an issue with his running between the wickets, the number of dot balls he consumed, and said he won't even bring up his fielding ability when asked for his reasons by the selector representing this particular player's zone. He had very objective and pointed explanations for each of his specific concerns about this player. About his running between the wickets, Dhoni is learnt to have said that he couldn't be sure whether that batsman would complete the run or stop in between, and such indecisiveness would have a negative effect on his partner's mindset. When pointed out that the batsman didn't have a bad strike rate by the prevailing standards, then Dhoni, never a big believer in numbers, is learnt to have said, '*Char* dot balls, last two balls *pe ek* boundary, *ek* single or double, strike rate *ho gaya* 90. (Four dot balls. A boundary and one or two runs on the last two balls. That takes the strike rate to 90.) The number of dot balls is the problem with this stat.' And true to his word, he didn't speak a word about his fielding. Eventually, the batsman in question wasn't picked for the squad and never played ODIs for India again. But when India found themselves in a tight spot during one of the matches in the tournament, Dhoni used the axing he'd engineered to motivate or send a quiet warning to his players. 'I want to say only this. I've dropped a lot of big players to bring you guys in. *Abhi kuch karna padega aap logon ko.* (You guys have to do something now.)' As always, a man of few words. India, of course, went on to win that game and the tri-series, the first time they'd won a tournament Down Under since 1985 when they had won the World Series.

'How can you give away a rank as prestigious as that to a cricketer, while we've earned and achieved it through our sweat and blood? What has he done for the army?' That's a question that is asked a lot about most honorary military officers by those who actually serve the country on the frontline. It's a valid one too. No civilian or even a Bollywood star has yet received an honorary Test cap from the BCCI after all, just for argument's sake even if the comparison might not be a direct fit.

Col Shankar admits that the sense of antipathy towards their high-profile celebrity inductee doesn't arise from envy. It has instead got more to do with Dhoni not being one to overtly promote the armed forces; he does it more subtly and at times anonymously—especially in financial matters—without beating a single drum, unlike others of his ilk.

'If they are not able to meet him, or they have introduced themselves as army officers and haven't been given an audience with him, they feel like he's not living up to the expectations. They don't know the kind of work he does. They think that he should spend crores on the army widows. "*Siachen mein ek banda mar gaya, uske liye kuch nahi kiya, ek tweet bhi nahin?* (A soldier dies in Siachen, he doesn't do anything, not even one tweet?)," they ask. For him, it matters more to speak to a jawan and find out more. He feels it's about leadership and not showmanship,' says Col Shankar.

It does makes sense why his detractors would think that Dhoni isn't doing enough, considering the present political climate of the country, where social media has become the platform and the pulpit to emblazon and preach about your patriotism even if it borders on jingoism. The fact that Dhoni doesn't toe this line, leads to the misconception that he doesn't care, and is only there to reap the benefits of holding a senior rank. So much so that some officers get annoyed when they hear that Dhoni is visiting their unit.

'The perception completely changes for anyone who's met him even for ten minutes. They're like *hamare type ka banda hai, yaar . . .* (he's like us). And within minutes after him leaving, their WhatsApp profile pictures have changed from the tricolour to M.S. Dhoni. That's his impact,' says Col Shankar laughing before listing out the various Dhoni contributions to the army, including lakhs of rupees spent on widows and martyr families.

Dhoni chooses subtler ways of promoting the army. It's become such a routine to see some part of Dhoni's apparel depicting or representing the army. He'll have those army fatigues on while travelling or even otherwise. His wicketkeeping gloves are custom-designed under his own supervision and carry a military theme and a name that resonates with it, MSD Warrior. His kitbag has had the fatigues' theme for a few years now, and is now popular among other cricketers too, both among those who play for India at the highest level and in the suburbs of Mumbai and Delhi who play for their local clubs.

More often than not, it's a direct statement in support of the army rather than having anything to do with fashion. Col Shankar says it's Dhoni's way of giving back to the army, at least in terms of exposure. 'He does it because he feels that people will notice. If not the fatigues, he'll have T-shirts with telltale signs. Then they'll ask, why and what is written? "Why does it say Airborne? What is Airborne?" He says when I wear it, people take a lot of pictures and post them, so at least that way the goodwill will spread.'

Dhoni has his own theory, not surprisingly, about why the army needs to be promoted more, or the air around it cleared as much as possible. He wants people to see how the soldiers live off the land in the border areas and the kind of sacrifices they make rather than simply relying on newspaper headlines, which brings us to his pet peeve. 'Why is it that when an army guy does something wrong, his profession is always mentioned in the headline like, say, "Ex-army did this and that", but when a lawyer or journalist does it, they just put a name and never bring his profession into disrepute?' Dhoni would ask the colonel repeatedly. The army, Dhoni is said to believe, is always put on a pedestal because they're expected to have an unreasonable level of moral uprightness, and as a result, any negative news about them alters the rest of the country's opinion of them greatly. And it's this reason that pushes him to try and promote the positives of the army to a greater extent.

The helicopter shot is synonymous with M.S, Dhoni, despite the fact that it wasn't originally his creation or the fact that he seems out of touch with it these days. But he's never quite lost touch with his expertise on helicopters— at one glance, he can identify its make. He uses this shrewdly to create a shock-effect, especially when he's around someone from the military. Col Shankar recalls the time he was taken to South Africa for a tour and how Dhoni just saw a copter take off from the airfield next to the one where they were waiting to board a flight, and immediately identified exactly which one it was. Just like that, and not for the first or the last, he'd left the colonel shaking his head in disbelief.

It's a unique skill that he's developed mainly through his natural powers of observation and also due to his insatiable inquisitiveness. He puts it to full use and ends up being a de-facto intelligence gatherer whenever he's on an away tour. The security officials assigned to the Indian team generally happen to be former military guys. Dhoni's modus operandi is to start a conversation about their weapon and make an observation or two about it.

'The guy will look at him with raised eyebrows and say, "How come you know about it?" He'll then tell him about his love for weapons. Then they'll bond over how both of them are a part of their country's special forces, and the conversation will drift towards comparing the kind of weapons each country possesses in its arsenal,' says Col Shankar. Whatever information is gathered is then duly passed on to the colonel, but always with a rider, 'Sir, if South Africa can have this and this weapon, why don't we have it?' That leaves the colonel speechless, with only a sheepish grin to show.

Dhoni the cricketer has never been known to obsess or even get hooked to the finer details of batting or wicketkeeping techniques. He's got a very Frank Sinatra 'I do it my way' approach to both. In later years, he has done work with video analysts to fine-tune certain aspects of his batting, but it's been more need-based and more to do with alignment without getting too pedantic over the nitty-gritties. I remember him telling a video analyst who was working with his technique during the tenth edition of the IPL: 'Sir, I've just woken up and had some chai; give me a few balls and the bat will come down the way you want it to.'

However, he's known to get very technical while handling a weapon, and according to Col Shankar, will keep shifting the gun around in his hand to find out the best way to hold it so that it fires at its optimum.

For, as Col Shankar puts it, he's always looking to tinker around even with day-to-day objects and see if they can be put to any unconventional use. It could range from using a mobile phone as a projectile to using a phone charger to make toast—the more extreme the better. Even with weapons, he spends a good deal of time talking about how they could be modified.

No wonder then that he keeps putting up Instagram videos of opening up his bikes and putting them back together like they are Lego pieces. It's got a lot to do with his very fauji principle of never calling room service for any aid and 'using the resources available to fix any problem'. It could be a pen that's stuck or even a sole that's come loose. Dhoni will not let anyone call for help, and take ten minutes to figure something out, whether it's using a shoe lace or a safety pin or anything. It's again something that's achieved by practising daily. This is an ingenuity that comes through in every facet of his cricket too, which the world has gotten used to by now. And you believe it's some form of raw urge that he needs to constantly get his hands to produce something out of nothing. This is often seen in his batting, where Dhoni, who, apart from being a hands-on captain, also tends to be very 'hands-on' in his batting, as his hands often do more work than his feet—especially the way he drives the ball through the covers where the wrists take over completely at the point of contact and would find gaps through packed off-side fields.

Meetings between Dhoni and the colonel are, of course, mainly centred around him going: 'Sir, aur batao na. Uss mission mein kya hua? (Sir, tell me more, no. What happened on that mission)?' or 'China ne aisa kar diya, sir, South China Sea mein. Bhutan mein kya ho raha hai, sir?

(China did that in the South China Sea. What's happening in Bhutan?)'

Over time, Col Shankar has realized that Dhoni has a penchant for the unconventional. This is reflected in the faujis he calls friends—'guys who are different', as the colonel puts it—or when it comes to civilians, even journalists. It's the same when it comes to army missions. 'War is too organized for his liking. Even army operations, where things are clear, with planned attacks, don't really get him going. Conventional things don't attract him. What he really gets fascinated by are cross-border attacks where information is scarce and soldiers often have to go against the norm to succeed,' says Col Shankar. But, of course—to steal a Dhoni catchphrase—there are questions that need to be answered too. '"Suppose the information that has come our way is wrong, what do we do? What are the contingency plans?" These are tactical and strategic questions that all young officers ask when they are coming up the ranks. So does MS,' the colonel adds.

Nothing, though, quite excites him as much as finding himself in a scenario where he needs to make contingency plans. There was the Delhi hotel fire, of course, but Col Shankar recalls another instance a few years ago. Dhoni had been invited for an event where many people were expected to gather. He was concerned about a potential melee upon his arrival. So, he came up with a strategy. With just 2 km to go for the venue, Dhoni told Col Shankar and his driver that they'd all have to switch places in the car. 'Ek kaam karte hai. (Let's do one thing.) I will drive from here. You sit next to me and we'll ask the driver to sit in the back,' were Dhoni's orders to the colonel. Dhoni's view was that as soon as those awaiting his arrival see a car, they would naturally look for Dhoni in the back seat, not find him and think he's not here yet.

'He said, "You wear a cap. People will look at you and say no, no, he's too dark." Nobody will look at the driver's seat,"' recalls Col Shankar. The plan worked to perfection, not surprisingly.

6

The Mahi Way

'Dhoni sir, I want to be India's next astronaut. They're planning to choose one now. I've been a test pilot and have completed many hours of flying. I'm the right guy. Please, please have a word with Sunita Williams. She's also a naval officer just like me. If you speak to her, they'll select me.' All along this plea, Dhoni simply kept nodding as if he was agreeing with every word the officer was saying to him.

Back in the car on their way out, Dhoni would ask Col Shankar, '*Sir, yeh Sunita Williams kaun hai?* (Who is this Sunita Williams?)' The colonel recalls being shocked and he spent the next couple of minutes raving about who Williams was, citing all her achievements in space and also, more crucially, how she was of Gujarati origin and a Padma Bhushan winner. As calmly as before, Dhoni's response to that was: '*Mera kya lena–dena usse, sir?* (What do I have to do with her, sir?)' Col Shankar had no option but to give up.

'Sunita Williams kaun hai?' Col Shankar says to me, laughs loudly and then continues, 'That poor chap came thinking that Dhoni will know everyone in the world and one word from him will send him to space.'

It wasn't the first time that Dhoni was shocking his friend with his complete ignorance about someone the colonel considered a famous personality. Often, the colonel would brag about having scored the autograph of a renowned sportsperson whom he had tracked down after plenty of effort, and all he would get in response was a '*Yeh kaun hai, sir?* (Who is this, sir?)' This happened most recently on the eve of the ODI team's departure to South Africa. The colonel met Dhoni in his hotel room in Mumbai. India had just commenced the third and what would turn out to be an infamous Test against the Proteas at the Wanderers in Johannesburg. As young pace sensation Lungi Ngidi ran in to bowl and took a wicket, Col Shankar would tell him about how his celebrations were very reminiscent of former West Indies pacer Patrick Patterson. The colonel then narrated Patterson's tragic tale, about how he had been a recluse for twenty-five years. And after listening and nodding throughout, Dhoni had the same response for him: 'Kaun tha, sir, woh? (Who was that, sir?) Never heard of him.'

It's not, however, a case of Dhoni being a snob about what and who came before him or being disrespectful towards celebrities from other fields. It's just a case of him 'not bothering about anything that doesn't affect him', as Col Shankar puts it.

'His ignorance was as remarkable as his knowledge.' No, this is not Col Shankar raving about his friend again.

That's Dr John Watson summing up his good friend Sherlock Holmes in *A Study in Scarlet*, the first of their adventures. In the novel, the good doctor, like the good colonel here, is astonished at how Holmes is not only ignorant of famous philosophers and theories; he also claims to not know that the earth travels around the sun or what constitutes the solar system. It is then that the foremost detective in the world— made so real by Arthur Conan Doyle—dishes out his famous theory about the mind being an 'empty attic' with no 'elastic walls': 'A fool takes in all the lumber of every sort that he comes across, so that the knowledge which might be useful to him gets crowded out, or best is jumbled up with a lot of other things . . . for every addition of knowledge you forget something that you knew before. It is of the highest importance, therefore, not to have useless facts elbowing out the useful ones.'

Now, I'm not saying that Dhoni isn't aware of the solar system or the earth's axis. If anything, I'm rather confident he is well aware of it, though I doubt he's been quizzed on it much. But what Holmes and Dhoni seem to have in common is this belief that they're better off not bothering with that which doesn't affect them.

Cricketers, the Indian ones in particular, often live in bubbles wherein they know little about what lies beyond their worlds. That's the reason why many of them often struggle with life after retirement. A rather renowned former Indian cricketer, for example, is said to still get flustered while checking himself in at airports because he spent nearly half his life being checked in by someone else. Some other Indian cricketers only find out what a supermarket actually looks like on the rare chance that they get to play county cricket or an international tour. I once encountered a modern-day Indian star in a supermarket in Antigua as he walked around clueless, looking for a deodorant. I eventually had to direct him towards the aisle which had a board that said 'Deodorants and Antiperspirants'. He looked back at me like I'd just reinvented the wheel.

Dhoni, however, seems to be an exception. You can't imagine him being lost after he's done with playing cricket. He's kind of ensured he's stayed on the periphery all through his career. Some close to him believe that he'll just disappear and perhaps become the character Phansukh Wangdu of *3 Idiots* once he retires from the game for good.

They also talk about his pointed and poignant views on Indian politics. He's someone who's known to be always aware of elections in various states and once even surprised a friend of his in Mumbai with his knowledge of the upcoming municipality elections in the city. He is known to have vehemently dismissed the theory, posed to him once by another friend, that if a superstar celebrity, of whom there is no dearth in India, decides to become a politician, he or she would win hands down regardless of which constituency he contests from—for example, a player from Mumbai choosing to contest from Bengaluru. Dhoni's response, I'm told, was that the celebrity in question would lose by a massive margin if he were to do so. The best way out instead, he believes, is to pick a place where people can connect to the person they're voting for in all aspects— language, caste, everything. That it's often the surname and not the name that matters in these cases.

He's also built up to be rather perspicacious about people—which we've established already through the several anecdotes from Chittu and Chhotu. But Col Shankar insists it's the same when it comes to analysing trends amongst people, regardless of how old or young they are.

'He psychoanalyses people a lot, like he has this theory about his really young fans. He believes that small girls tend to be more open and uninhibited while asking him questions as compared to little boys. "Outside the room the boy would have said, I'll ask him this and that, but as soon as he enters the room, *dekho*, sir, he'll just stand there and not ask a single question," MS used to tell me. And I saw it happen too, just like he said it did. These little girls just walk in and start asking him the most personal of questions,' says Col Shankar. Dhoni is known to appreciate people who are upfront and direct. A journalist who has grown close to him over the years reveals, 'When he'd come to my house in Pune for lunch once, my daughters innocently asked Mahi about how he met Sakshi. And he sat and told them the whole love story.'

The Dhoni family—including the dogs and the various vehicles—have now moved and fully settled into their new farmhouse on Ranchi's Ring Road. But when I was in Ranchi visiting Chittu and coach Banerjee, Sakshi and Chittu had been still overseeing the final touches to the farmhouse. Chittu would constantly be pulled away from our meetings to attend to his responsibilities at the farmhouse. I asked him once how often he and Dhoni talk while he is away on his long foreign tours.

Chittu didn't need to think too hard. He explained that phone calls from his oldest friend are few and far between. '*Farmhouse ka kaam kaisa chal raha hai poochne phone karega.* (He'll call to know about the work on the farmhouse.) But the calls are very short and to the point.' And without me asking, Chittu had a theory why that's the case, one that he declared with great conviction, as always.

'If he's in England, Mumbai *bhool gaya. Mumbai gaya toh Ranchi bhool gaya. Woh jahaan hai, woh waheen hai.* (When he's in England, he forgets about Mumbai. When he's in Mumbai, Ranchi is forgotten. He's present wherever he is.) At that point, nothing else matters to him. That's why everyone says he lives in the present.' If true, then it kind of adds some gravitas to his peculiar, even infamous, comment on the New Zealand tour of 2009 about getting ready for a Test in Napier only eighteen hours after arriving in the city.

'When it comes to the mind, it depends on what you're feeding into the mind. You come and say, "This is Napier" and it believes it's Napier. If you see, it's an abstract. When people say, "He's in form," nobody has seen form. It's a state of mind,' Dhoni had said to a stunned media audience.

This was perhaps a window into Dhoni's real state of mind even if at that time it may have seemed like he was deflecting a question. It is in tune with his trademark efforts at disassociating the answer to a question during press conferences to such an extent that nobody, including the person who asked it, would remember the original question.

Another time Dhoni would kind of snap at a reporter (this was in 2014 at Brisbane) when he was asked about why he, as captain, had persisted with the short-ball ploy against the Aussie lower-order despite India being in a strong position. 'First of all,' Dhoni replied, 'you don't really know what was going on in my mind and so don't speculate as to what was going on in my mind, just leave that to me.'

That ability to stay in the present perennially manages to amaze people. It is a state of mind that perhaps even Sherlock Holmes is not known to have possessed, at least not without help from his pipe. For, to be truly in the present, like everyone around him claims he always has been, you require an extreme form of surrealism, almost to separate your subjective from the objective and somehow find an in-between place where you are totally one with the present. In Dhoni's case, according to Col Shankar, it's derived from that other MS Principle, which is about 'controlling the controllables'.

In the army, for instance, soldiers realize the implication of staying in the present mainly when they don't know what's coming next. How much ever they are taught about it in training, to follow the diktat of not losing sight of the aim and believing that the casualty will be taken care of— even if one of your comrades has been shot dead right next to you—requires that kind of detachment.

'If you fret about that guy, you might get hit and there'll be more casualties. The operation will get affected. So you have to keep moving on. That's why in the air force what they do is, if there's a crash, immediately, all the aircraft take off to say that, we just have to carry on,' explains Col Shankar. Dhoni though, the colonel insists, already had this trait much before his tryst with the uniform. 'It's like some sadhu thing to say but difficult to practise. But he does it.'

Those close to him in Ranchi recall numerous incidents when they had seen their beloved friend put this into practice. And they all agree that the reason he's able to do that is rather straightforward. 'Because the future is planned in his head, he can afford to live in the present. We're not surprised by any decision he takes, like the rest of the world. *Uske pet mein rehta hai.* (It remains with him.) Nobody else knows. It's only after he takes a decision that you'll be like, wow, how long did he have that in his head,' says Chittu.

There was, however, one occasion when even Chittu was left stupefied by Dhoni. It happened in 2010 when one day, he was asked to fly immediately to Delhi with no reason given. When he reached Delhi, he was asked to get himself to Dehradun. A confused Chittu followed the orders and only when he reached Dehradun did he realize that his schoolmate was getting married the next day. 'The only thing he told me was, *tu chal* (you come). He'd kept it such a low-key affair to avoid the media frenzy that even I was not privy to the information,' he says.

'He's able to savour every moment and relish it more than others, whether it is good or bad, because *woh saas leta rehta hai* (he keeps breathing). You notice him, he'll always take deep breaths despite being the fittest cricketer in the country as if he wants to make the most of everything, rather than rushing through life like most of us do,' says another friend.

Coach Banerjee recounts that when Dhoni was playing for the CCL, he would be paid Rs 1500 as stipend. He would somehow manage his entire month's expenditure with that money. He never worried about the struggle. He never once seemed to think even a step beyond the one he was taking at that moment, but still managed to be a few steps ahead of the rest—like he can often do on the field even now.

'It was his thing from a young age. He never believed or thought that one thing will lead to another. He knew there was a path to take, a process to follow. If he was batting in a match, he was only concerned about the ball coming at him. Even if the selectors were there watching, he didn't think about if I score here, I'll catch their attention,' the coach says.

'Forget about the 1500 during his CCL days. He used to come back to Ranchi from his railways job with Rs 100 and still spend that on us, his close friends. He never bothered about whether he'll have anything left. Today, he's probably smarter than any other Indian cricketer when it comes to investing money. And his *shauk* (love) is bikes and cars, and he indulges. He has every right to. He's enjoying this moment now,' Chittu adds.

Another friend, slightly older than the rest, but whose home he visits rather often whenever he's in his town, reveals how Dhoni can take the whole 'living in the present' bit to extreme levels.

'Whenever he comes home for food, he doesn't bring his phone along. He leaves it at the hotel. Two and a half hours he'll sit at my place. Such an important and busy man without his phone, and we'll all be amazed. He will sense our astonishment and simply dismiss it, saying, "Nothing can be so urgent that I need my phone at all times. Everything can wait,'" the friend says. I've heard Dhoni himself talk about his pet peeve—people peering into their phones when they're being spoken to or when they're amidst a group of people. It apparently annoys him far more than most other modern-day distractions. This exemplifies his friends' belief that despite being a gadget freak, he ensures he never becomes a slave to them.

Dhoni isn't known to be staunchly religious but visits the Deori temple—or 'Dhoni-wala temple', as Tripadvisor.in lists it—almost every time he's in the city before or after a tour. Chittu is generally in tow, and in his various visits to one of Ranchi's most iconic spots, he's observed another facet of Dhoni that is again linked with his carpe-diem approach to life.

'*Haath kisiko nahi dikhata.* (He has never shown his palm to a fortune teller.) He never even extends it towards an astrologer. He'll have the same dialogue always. "*Achcha naseeb hai, chalne do.* (My luck is good, let it keep going.)"'

Kiran More, former India wicketkeeper, has known Dhoni for a long time. He'd first come across him in 2004 when Dhoni was taking apart a quality North Zone attack in Chandigarh. More was there as the chairman of the senior selection committee. It was love at first sight. A bond was formed and it continues to this day. So much so that Dhoni would ask for More to train actor Sushant Singh Rajput to not just bat and keep like Dhoni, but be Dhoni for the movie.

It was More who gave Dhoni a break into the Indian team as the chairman of selectors fourteen years ago. He was also at the selection committee meeting six months later when the then India coach Greg Chappell proclaimed to his shocked audience that 'Dhoni was a future India captain'. It took less than two years for Chappell's words to come true—when Dhoni became India's first-ever captain at the World T20 tourney before becoming India's captain across all formats just over a year later.

Dhoni's style of captaincy has won him many complimentary sobriquets, but More uses one that I'd never heard in this context, of him having led the team like a corporate chief. It took me a while to fathom exactly why he sounded so convinced about it.

'He is a corporate guy who understands the workmen, the production guys, the marketing guys and the finance team. That's why Dhoni is a complete package,' he says. Earthy and ingenious are likelier or commoner descriptions of India's most successful captain of all time. It came to the fore, More says, when Dhoni was thrust into the role of the captain of the T20 squad. That was when all the senior players had backed out—perhaps because they didn't necessarily fathom the scope of T20 cricket back then—and the young captain was left with a motley crew of mostly untested, raw talent. Most of Ranchi still believes strongly that it was a set-up for him to fail. Kiran More, though, recalls it having left Dhoni in a position wherein he had nothing to lose but absolutely everything to gain. The radical decision was taken by More's successor, Dilip Vengsarkar. More not only considers it to be a masterstroke but also believes that it helped Indian cricket turn the corner.

'The factory's sick unit was given to him, and the sick unit was converted into a profit-making company. That's what Dhoni did at that World T20,' More says.

It makes sense too. When you look at his captaincy reign overall, Dhoni has been the best CEO a company could ask for, not just bringing the best out of his resources by assigning them well-suited roles but also being able to be always on top of things.

'But his journey was different once he took over as Test and ODI captain. Before that, he was a general manager with around seven to eight CEOs in the team, all former India captains or superstars in their own right—Tendulkar, Dravid, Ganguly, Sehwag, Laxman, Bhajji (Harbhajan Singh), Zaheer Khan, Nehra, to name a few. And overnight he gets promoted to being the MD and suddenly he has to look after all those CEOs,' More says. Dhoni took over as ODI captain for the seven-match series against Australia in September 2007. He provided a telling indicator to the era of surprises that Indian cricket was embarking on by pulling out left-arm spinner Murali Kartik, who'd been in the Neo Sports studio as an expert, and picking him as a replacement for Ramesh Powar after the first three ODIs. For the record, Kartik notched up figures of 6/27, the best figures for a left-arm spinner in ODIs, in the last match at Mumbai.

One of Dhoni's prime captaincy traits is to define not just his own responsibilities but also the roles of those playing under him. And it's not just on the field. Dhoni has a defined role for everyone around him. Like with most of his other attributes, this one too he practises in his daily life with the same earnestness.

'Everyone, including his wife, his parents, his friends, his agents and his employers, has a fixed role in his life and each has a line that he or she knows they cannot cross. Sakshi cannot go overboard by saying anything about his parents or me. The same goes for his parents (they cannot say anything against Sakshi). At the same time, I cannot say a word out of line about Sakshi or his cricket. He would also stand up for me in front of anyone,' Chittu had said when I met him in Ranchi.

He'd also recalled an incident when a JSCA official once insulted Chittu at the Ranchi stadium. When it reached Dhoni's ears, he wasn't pleased. When he visited the stadium next—which apparently, Dhoni does every day when he's in Ranchi—he confronted the association official. Chittu recalled with pride how Dhoni sorted the man with just one line: '*Chai se garam toh kettle hi hota hai, sir*. (Sir, the kettle is always hotter than the tea.)' The official apparently never looked into Chittu's eyes again. He had learnt his lesson. 'Mahi knows I have a temper but if Mahi's clear that I'm not in the wrong, then whoever says anything to me will definitely get a piece of his mind,' he had added. Chittu and Co. have also realized a long time ago that despite often bursting with ideas and suggestions regarding their friend's cricketing career, it's best not to bring them up when Dhoni's around. For, the response generally is nothing more than '*rehne do*' (let it be). Having spent some time with Chittu, I'm rather impressed that he actually manages to show restraint and not voice the strong opinions he has about those making life difficult for his friend.

In October 2017, Ziva, just two and a half years' old, turned YouTube sensation after a video of her singing a famous Malayalam song, '*Ambalapuzha Unnikannanodu Nee*' went viral, and the little girl even got an invite from the Ambalapuzha temple to pay a visit. It was later revealed that she had learnt it from her Malayali nanny, Sheila Aunty. The song—it received nearly 400,000 views within the first week of it surfacing—apart, Ziva is also known to speak quite a bit of Malayalam. And most others around Ziva are known to talk to her in English. Dhoni realized last year that this meant that his parents didn't quite know how to communicate with their granddaughter. So, a decision was taken that both Sakshi and Ziva—who, otherwise, tend to accompany him on most tours, at least for certain periods anyway—would stay back in Ranchi during the one and a half months of the IPL in 2017.

Those close to Dhoni reveal that he wanted Ziva to get used to being around her grandparents more. They also laud Sakshi's decision to stay back. She's a celebrity wife and would have her own aspirations, but she was prepared to put them on the back-burner. Dhoni has also taken on the role of teaching Ziva the ropes of Indian culture, including touching the feet of any elderly person she meets. For the record, Sakshi did make an appearance during last year's IPL.

She went on Instagram in defence of her husband after Harsh Goenka, whose brother owned Rising Pune Supergiant, the team that Dhoni played for in 2016 and 2017, expressed a few highly critical views on the former India captain after he was replaced as the franchise captain by Steve Smith. Sakshi first posted a picture wearing a Chennai Super Kings helmet with a hashtag of '#throwback' on Instagram and then followed it up with a quotation about karma.

'When a bird is alive, it eats ants. When the bird is dead, ants eat the bird. Time and circumstances can change at any time. Don't devalue or hurt anyone in life. You may be powerful today, but remember, time is more powerful than you. One tree makes a million matchsticks but only one match is needed to burn a million trees. So be good and do good.' One would think that it was directed at Goenka, but was done with the kind of subtlety that perhaps even Dhoni would envy. I couldn't quite find out the exact origins of the quote but at least the first couple of lines could easily have been—as any journalist who's attended a Dhoni press conference would concur—out of the Dhoni book of 'how to raise eyebrows at a media gathering'. Birds, ants and the irony of who eats whom. Yes, they sound very Dhoni-esque. Sakshi and Ziva, by the way, have been as omnipresent on and off the field as Dhoni himself during his 2018 IPL campaign where he's returned as CSK's captain.

Dhoni loves to post videos of his dogs, the other love of his life. He once famously stated that they are his most non-judgemental and dispassionate supporters. 'I have three dogs at home. Even after losing a series or winning a series, they treat me the same way,' he has said. These roles are not defined in a dictatorial fashion wherein those around Dhoni are in any way meant to be subservient to him. There is no hierarchy in place here just because he's the famous one. His close ones respect his candour in these interpersonal relationships because he remains impartial and objective, and doesn't define these roles as if he'd learnt them in some business management school. The human touch is all too evident in every Dhoni relationship. Stories abound of how the door of his room is always left open so that any player can seek him out for a chat, or a PlayStation challenge. He's proven over and over again to be a captain who wants to know about his players' backgrounds, and hear their stories. The most significant reason he gets so much love from the people who know him is that he plays his role in their lives to perfection.

The only other sportsperson of his generation who has managed his personal and professional lives so that they coexist seamlessly and sans fuss is Roger Federer. There are some glaring similarities in the way these two great sportsmen view life.

In an interview to *Sports Illustrated* in 2014, Federer spoke about not enjoying being alone and how he loved having an 'open house at his hotel so that people can gather'. He said that he gave his coach and physio the key to his room so that they could drop in whenever. There's also the part where the tennis legend described his fling with social media and called it the 'biggest change' in his off-field persona. Federer, like Dhoni for most parts of his career, led his personal life behind the proverbial fourth wall. They were performers of the highest quality but liked to keep a cap on how much the world really knew about them beyond their prodigious performances. They were cerebral and clinical in victory and defeat, even if Federer could, at times, be temperamental on court, regardless of whether he was winning or losing. In later years of course, he would debunk the theory that 'boys don't cry' and become the poster boy for letting one's emotions flow down one's cheeks, after almost every Grand Slam victory. They are champions who ooze coolness but somehow make their life beyond the stadia seem rather normcore.

Social media allowed both Dhoni and Federer to create windows, or slight indentations at least, in that fourth wall and provide the odd glimpse into the real lives they led behind the curtain of immeasurable success. 'If I do it, it needs to be me. My idea was to give people extra insight nobody else has,' is what Federer told *Sports Illustrated* about being on social media. He might as well have been speaking on Dhoni's behalf. For, Dhoni generally only uses social media to provide rare 'insights' and glimpses into his real life and his real passions—bikes, dogs, family, military. Federer, of course, gets to showcase the wonderful amalgamation between his personal and professional life a lot more, being the foremost champion at an individual sport, which means for two weeks at a stretch, during most Grand Slams, he's constantly dabbling in both for the camera.

Dhoni, of course, opened up his life to the world when he became the first active cricketer to have a movie made about his life. Untold or not, those were stories that you wouldn't have expected someone as private as Dhoni to put forth to the world. You could call it his marketing acumen or his foresight. Like most of his gambles on the field, the decision to air his life story on the big screen seemed to be a calculated one. It was the equivalent of finishing off a bowler's spell when he's in great rhythm and taking wickets in every other over rather than holding back a portion of his quota for the death. The idea would have been to make the movie at a time when people could watch it and relate it with the real Dhoni actively doing what he does best. Why wait and have people recall your feats retrospectively? It was a master stroke.

'He might not have studied much. But his IQ, *baap re baap*, is of another level. He taps into market trends like nobody's business and is always five steps ahead. See how he uses social media so smartly by letting his fans get a piece of him that would never be possible through the mainstream media. At the same time, he'll be aware of everything that's happening in the country. Suddenly, he will ask about the BMC election in Mumbai,' says More.

'If he wants to, he can be a master at keeping a low profile. I remember two years ago he attended a wedding in Baroda and nobody found out. Only the CISF (Central Industrial Security Force) guy at the airport was informed. He landed and they whisked him away. He went for the wedding, spent half hour there chatting with everyone, stayed overnight, and the next morning, he was off. Just like that,' he adds.

Understanding your role and your place in Dhoni's life is something that those who are allowed to enter his very tiny inner circle get used to rather quickly. Col Shankar knows that there are times when Dhoni wants him around and times when he doesn't. And he makes it rather obvious.

'He just doesn't answer his house phone in his hotel room, ever. And he knows I know that. Somehow, I don't know how, but when he wants me in his room, he somehow always picks up the house phone when the reception folk call to check with him. He'll say later, "See, I knew you would be calling,"' says Col Shankar.

The same formula works in their phone conversations too. The colonel, the irrepressible cricket fan, is never shy about sending a slew of messages ranging from 'well done', 'what a great stumping' and 'other silly stuff', as he puts it, to Dhoni, messages which never ever evoke a response of any sort, smiley or otherwise. But here's where Col Shankar gets to see the other side of Dhoni's penchant to have roles for everyone, which is an uncanny knack for knowing who needs to be given importance when.

'When I became a colonel, after having been a lieutenant colonel just like him, I said, "MS, you have to salute me now." I picked up the rank in the morning at around nine, and that evening I got a message. Same-day reply is very rare. He must be having 1000 friends in the army, and 10,000 others send him WhatsApp messages. For him to realize it's an important day for me, and despite so many WhatsApp messages, to send me a congratulatory message is just extraordinary,' says Shankar.

It happened again this year, in which time Shankar had, of course, sent another hundred cricket-related messages which had no response. It was the day the colonel had decided to hang up his boots.

'I said today is my last day, and he immediately said, "Welcome to the retired gang." That time he was in Kashmir, in the midst of everything, very busy. Every moment is busy.

He understood that those two days were important for me,'
he adds. There has been one time, though, the first and only
so far, when Dhoni himself initiated a conversation over
WhatsApp with the colonel. It happened the day the Indian
army carried out cross-border attacks into Pakistan.

'He messaged asking for the numbers of those guys. I
said, "They won't have telephones now but I'll get them
for you." He got through to some people and said, "Well
done, we are proud of you." Look at the motivation the
chief officer would have had after M.S. Dhoni's call. He
understands what is important in life, which is a rare quality.'

'I thought after playing for India he'll change . . . I thought after
2007 World T20, he'll change . . . I thought after marriage
he'll change . . . *ab toh badlega* (now he'll change) . . . ab toh
badlega . . . But no, nothing. So by the time the 2011 World
Cup win came, I knew *yeh kabhi nahi badlega* (he'll never
change) . . .' Chittu says with almost a sense of resignation.
The more things changed, the more Dhoni stayed the same.

On the cricket field, at least from around 2007 to 2015,
Dhoni seemed to be at the forefront of evolution. It was like
he was always faster on the uptake—in terms of limited overs
cricket anyway—of where the cricket world was headed.

The only facet of him that has changed comes as a
major surprise to me and it has to do with his cricket. In his
extensive career as ODI cricket's nerveless finisher, he has
thrived on taking run chases into the last over and setting up
what I have often referred to in my match reports as Dhoni
Time—basically, cricket's own Mexican standoff scenario

where the bowler and he are in a duel with their hands on their respective triggers. Till, say, a couple of years ago, you could almost bank on Dhoni firing the fatal blow and hitting bullseye like he does with weapon in hand. But it's not been the same ever since Kagiso Rabada bowled that sensational last over in Kanpur when the young South African pacer conceded only five runs with Dhoni and India needing 11 for victory. For good measure, Rabada told the press after the match about how he'd grown up watching Dhoni finish off matches and here he was getting the better of him.

He did seem to turn back the clock during the 2018 IPL in terms of his power-hitting and power-finishing. While Chennai Super Kings' third title win in their comeback season was the big story of the tournament's eleventh edition, a more charming postscript of their journey was how 'old' Dhoni had started batting like the Dhoni of old.

Some of the cricketers he grew up playing cricket with in Ranchi recall him having only one rule about run chases which shockingly was: 'Never take it till the last over. Finish it off before that.' Maybe Dhoni was still to discover his penchant for sudden death back then. (The other surprise is that he didn't always have this unabashed aversion to the media, but we'll come to that in the relevant chapter.)

'He has always been the same person' is a tribute to Dhoni you hear everywhere. Right from his MECON Colony mates to schoolmates to teammates to coaches, and even the security chief at the Ranchi stadium, everyone says that about him. Col Shankar reasons that Dhoni is able to be the same because of his two staunch principles in life—'control the controllables' and that 'no man can have everything in life, there's always that one thing you will never be able to have'.

'He can only control what is in his control. So that's all that bothers him. Like, if you get up and go right now while I'm talking, what can I do about it? It's a simple logic and easier said than followed. But he does it,' says Col Shankar. Dhoni's belief that no man can have everything in life is an interesting premise. It is almost like asking you to seek out that one thing you can never have and almost develop the confidence that you can achieve everything else, however unachievable it may seem.

In Dhoni's case, and I'm sticking my neck out here a little, it might well be about learning swimming—at least that's what Chittu implies. Apparently, Dhoni tried learning how to swim back in 2007 soon after the World T20 win in South Africa, and just couldn't master it. Maybe he has become better at it now, but Chittu recalls this as something that bothered him back then.

'I couldn't believe it. There was something that even Mahi couldn't learn well. Both Mahi and I had enrolled for lessons at the Birsa Club, but neither of us ever managed to go beyond the four-feet mark,' Chittu recalls. It's kind of funny that he makes this disclosure while we are next to the swimming pool at the JSCA stadium, after he's successfully thwarted the local swimming coach's attempts at getting him to give the pool another shot.

It was at the JSCA stadium that I got a very discernible glimpse into both Dhoni's magnanimity towards those he considers his people and the magnitude to which he's revered. Chittu introduced me to everyone as the author of this new book on Mahi and how he was showing me around. And wherever he took me, and at the JSCA stadium in particular, I was given an overwhelming reception.

'Sir, you are writing on our superstar. That makes you a superstar too. You are our guest of honour,' one official tells me. As flattering as it sounds, I'm taken aback simply by the enormity of the love that Dhoni enjoys in these parts. Though I refuse the same official's attempts at convincing me to stay back for a beer, he ensures that I get dropped back at my hotel in his fancy car, and he even opens the back door to usher me in for good measure. Superstar indeed.

Manoj-bhaiya, the security incharge at the JSCA stadium, whom Dhoni wishes on 1 January every year like I mentioned before, is a muscular and robust figure who never stops smiling. He turns guide for me and takes me around the facility where Dhoni spends three to four hours every day when he's in town. Nearly every room in the stadium offices has at least a couple of items—be it memorabilia or the exercise apparatus in the case of the gymnasium—that was donated by Dhoni. Manoj-bhaiya receives a forewarning about Dhoni's visit either from the man himself or from Chittu in the morning, and he immediately makes sure that the necessary measures are put in place for the man's arrival. Dhoni's schedule is rather fixed. An hour or so at the gym—at times with

Chittu in tow, and then most of the time is spent making fun of his paunch—followed by a game of pool in the billiards' room. And then if he's in the mood, Dhoni and Manoj-bhaiya set off for a few laps around the stadium. It's during these jogs that Dhoni shows his inquisitive side again, inquiring about Manoj-bhaiya's time in the military and his life in general.

Dhoni insisted on Manoj-bhaiya being with him in February 2017 when the former 'ticket collector' travelled in a train for the first time in thirteen years with the Jharkhand team for the Vijay Hazare Trophy in Kolkata— from Ranchi to Howrah. 'He was amazing. I stayed up all night despite all the necessary precautions having been put in place, and he too spent most of the time awake, making fun of the boys, telling them stories and chatting with me. He literally didn't sleep, I remember. And the next day when we disembarked, he went straight to the hotel and, I think, slept for the entire day,' Manoj-bhaiya tells me.

As the guided tour nearly comes to an end, Chittu points at an incomplete structure, say two-storey high and with foundations laid for what looks like rectangular rooms. '*Aur kitne din lagega, bhaiya?* (How many more days it will take to finish?),' he asks the security head. It's a small complex to house badminton courts, which Chittu tells me, are mainly being put in place for Mahi to indulge in his favourite pastime.

'The problem is whenever he comes here, he'll start playing there with someone or the other,' he says, pointing at an open space under the stands to the right of the pavilion area. 'It's really slippery there and we always get worried that he shouldn't slip and hurt himself. The JSCA guys anyway wanted a couple of badminton courts but thanks to Mahi they are getting it done earlier than planned,' says Chittu.

'I asked him for Reebok shoes. Lotto wala. He bought it himself. I still have it and wear it on and off. Keep cleaning and wearing it. *Yaadgaar hai.* (It's memorable.) He bought me the most expensive car I've had, a Scorpio. My first bike he gave,' Chittu lists away.

In his younger days, Chittu's house was Dhoni's getaway. Since his mother would be away at work, the flat was empty through the day and the two would spend time trying their hand in the kitchen and debating over whose chai-making skills were worse. The frequency of visits naturally reduced over time, but even now the only house Dhoni doesn't ever hesitate going to is Chittu's. There was one visit, however, that Chittu wasn't aware of, and that is what he considers the apotheosis of his friendship with Mahi.

'I used to run a business with a partner. At one point he duped me, and I lost a lot of money. I was at my wits' end and didn't know what to do. I was feeling a sense of shame too and didn't want to ask Mahi for help even though I knew I could. One of those days, I returned home dejectedly to find my mother looking very relaxed for a change. As soon as I entered, she said, "*Tu darr kyun raha hai, Mahi ne aake bola hai sab theek kar dega woh.* (Why are you afraid; Mahi came and said he will set everything right.)" I started sobbing because I couldn't believe he had gone directly and met my mother without informing me,' he says.

When Mahi comes visiting his home, Chittu says no lavish arrangements have to be made. 'Despite having reached such a stature, he's got no *ghammand* (arrogance). *Usko bolo, neeche baitho, baith jaayega . . . . jo khaana do, kha lega . . . koi naatak nahi hai . . . Suljha hua hai bahut andhar se.* (If you ask him to sit on the floor, he'll sit on the floor. He'll eat whatever you've prepared, without a fuss. He's a very sorted person.)'

7

A Captain Comes into His Own

In February 2008, India were chasing down a facile total of 160 against Australia in the Commonwealth Bank Series at the Melbourne Cricket Ground (MCG). It was only the fifteenth ODI as captain for Dhoni, and he was at the crease with Rohit Sharma. With 10 runs to win, he called for a needless change of gloves. In cricket, it's generally with a pair of gloves that you see information arriving from the dressing room. Dhoni was doing the opposite though. He was sending a poignant message back to the pavilion. 'Nobody will celebrate on the balcony once we win this match.'

Meanwhile in the middle, Dhoni was handing down instructions to Rohit, on how the youngster should conduct himself while shaking hands with the Aussies once the match got over. He wanted it to be as tepid as possible. 'When they give their hand, just firmly hold yours out without folding it like an obligation, but don't overdo it. And just stare blankly at them without any hint of excitement.'

This was back when the Australians were still at their indomitable best. Beating them meant a big deal to any opposition, that too in their own backyard at the mighty MCG. It was a period when Ricky Ponting's team believed that every loss was an 'upset' and not just a win for their opponents. India had dominated this particular match from the beginning. Ishant Sharma, Sreesanth and Irfan Pathan had gathered nine wickets between them and shot out the hosts for just 159. India had more or less cruised to their target and now Dhoni the rookie wanted to give his all-conquering, world-beating counterpart his version of the cold shoulder.

'This was Mahi's way of saying it's no big deal. My bowlers got them all out for 160 and we are chasing it down, *usme kaunse badi baat hai* (there's no big deal in it). If we celebrate wildly, the Aussies will be vindicated in their belief that this was an upset. We wanted to tell them that this is not a fluke. This is going to happen over and over again. The Aussies simply couldn't handle it. They were shaken,' a player from that tour revealed much later.

That wasn't the only time during the Commonwealth Bank Series, which India eventually ended up winning, when Dhoni got the better of the Aussies at their own 'mental disintegration' game. Like he does with everything else, the Indian captain did it in his own style, without ever going overboard.

A few of the younger players in the team had told Dhoni that one of Australia's premier batsmen not known to hold back from expressing his thoughts about an opponent on the field, had been pressurizing and sledging every one of them when they were batting. And that when one responded in kind, the player asked the youngster to show him some respect. So, the next time he walked out to open the innings, Dhoni lined up all the juniors near the boundary line in a mock guard of honour. And all they kept saying to the burly Australian was, 'respect, respect, respect', as he walked towards the middle. 'It was Mahi's way of saying, "*Aapko maangke respect chahiye na. Yeh le lo respect.* (You want respect on demand. Here it is.),"' says a former teammate.

The one-day leg of this tour came at the heels of a tumultuous Test series which, in addition to the Monkeygate fiasco, had seen the two teams at each other's throats on and off the field. India felt robbed in Sydney when a few umpiring decisions, from Steve Bucknor in particular, went against them—this was six months before the birth of the decision review system (DRS). Anil Kumble, the Test captain, had left for home at the end of the Test series but not before declaring: 'Only one team is playing in the spirit of the game.' India won the next Test in Perth but lost the series.

Ponting and Co. were all set for an encore in the one-day series. Dhoni, still only into his fourth year of international cricket and on his first foreign assignment as captain in the ODIs, was left to face the heat. He did it his own way— he reduced the friction between the two sides by simply not reacting to any stimuli. The Aussies were flabbergasted. This was M.S. Dhoni's style of war without bloodshed. It worked, and in the end he had a trophy to show for it.

'*Goli maarta hai apne style mein.* (He shoots in his own style.) He says the problem is if I allow my boys to give *maa–behen ki gaali* (swear words involving someone's mother or sister); it's they and not the one being subjected to it who'll feel the pinch of what they've done for the rest of the day,' one of Dhoni's close friends explains.

'He doesn't believe in overt displays of aggression. He believes that if you want to hurt them, do it in your style, not in their way. If they believe in swearing, you don't need to do it,' he adds.

Incidentally, seven years and two tours later, Dhoni hadn't changed his opinion on the matter. In the 2014–15 Test series in Australia, which was riddled with incidents of players like Virat Kohli, David Warner and Brad Haddin being at each other's throats, Dhoni spoke about how he never held his players back from a confrontation, but only asked them never to get personal. It'd been his opinion throughout.

Dhoni wasn't just good at defusing tetchy situations with the opposing team. He could, at times, put his own teammates at ease in a tense scenario. Take the 2013 IPL final. Chennai Super Kings had been in the trenches. The spot-fixing saga was at its peak and throwing up names and scandals on a daily basis. Their team principal, who was later described as a 'cricket enthusiast', was out on bail. The team was under the pump. The players had been in a lockdown at the hotel.

As the CSK players prepared for the customary huddle near the boundary ropes, Dhoni sensed the tension around him. Vexed faces, local and foreign, all waiting for their captain to speak magic words of inspiration and motivation.

Dhoni stuck to his straight-faced approach. He said, 'Boys, we are second on the IPL Fair Play Award rankings. I want us to do everything we can to finish on top of that list. Good luck.' And he was off. Later, he told a teammate that it was his way of breaking the tension. But back in 2008, Indian cricket was just getting used to their new captain. He did things differently. He wasn't in-your-face like Ganguly or passive-aggressive like Dravid; he wasn't laid-back like Azharuddin or a genius expecting everyone else to be one, like Tendulkar; and he could never match Kumble for his intensity. He had his own ideas, and in all likelihood, more conviction than any other Indian captain before him, about his own ideas. You can say he might even have started a trend, looking at how Virat Kohli takes calls on and off the field.

Former Bihar and Jharkhand captain Tarique-ur-Rehman describes his one-time teammate's approach to captaincy, and maybe even life, perfectly: 'Mahi is convinced that his funda is the correct funda. More often than not, his fundas just come off.'

Nobody has quite acclimatized to the captaincy role as rapidly and unassumingly as Dhoni has in Indian cricket history. There might have been those who'd played fewer matches who got the job. But there was no precedent for a youngster who was still getting used to the attention that an India cricketer receives after being suddenly thrust with this significant burden.

T20 cricket comes in for a lot of flak around the world, and in India too. But India certainly does owe T20 cricket a huge debt. If there was no T20 cricket, and no reluctance on the part of the who's who of that generation to play the format, one wonders if Dhoni would have gotten that break and eventually ended up as the most successful Indian captain across all three versions of the game. Or imagine a scenario where even one of those seniors, whether it was Tendulkar or Dravid, had decided to go to South Africa. Would Dhoni have had the free hand that he enjoyed and relished during those dramatic two weeks which changed his life forever? For all his singular and awe-inspiring attributes, you can never quite ignore the right-time–right-place serendipity that tails the man.

He'd already shown streaks of opting for the unthinkable early in the tournament. It came during the league encounter between India and Pakistan which ended in a tie. For the bowl-out that followed, Pakistan chose their best bowlers while Dhoni's first three picks were Virender Sehwag, Harbhajan Singh and Robin Uthappa. At that point, it made no sense.

And while all three Pakistanis missed the target, the three Indians hit bullseye, including Uthappa. The young opener doffed his hat to the crowd too for good

measure. But in that instant, maybe Indian cricket was
doffing its hat too, to a new era, an era of expecting the
unexpected.

'I would have never even thought of giving it to Robin.
But that's what makes a leader. If you are scared of taking a
call, you can't be successful. You need guts to gamble,' says
Kiran More.

Go watch that video of the bowl-out once again.
And look out for Dhoni's positioning behind the stumps.
It's a great example of his situational awareness and his
understanding of the angles on the field.

He's kneeling right behind the stumps but not too far or
too close to them. It's the perfect distance where his width
and those of the stumps seem congruent when seen from
the bowling end. So, for Sehwag, Harbhajan and Uthappa,
Dhoni doesn't play the role of a keeper but adds almost an
extra dimension to the target in their sights. In this position,
he also ensures there's no distraction for the bowler. It's a
geometrical marvel.

You just have to see Kamran Akmal's position to
understand Dhoni's brilliance in this case. Akmal takes
his normal position, slightly to the right of off-stump,
for the likes of Umar Gul and Yasir Arafat. While Arafat
slips a full-toss outside off-stump, Gul ends up bowling
a beautiful length delivery that would have tempted a
right-hander, if there was one in position, into playing
at it.

Dhoni's decision to give Joginder Sharma the final over
of the World T20 final, with Misbah-ul-Haq on strike, is
always used to illustrate his ingenuity. That decision has

been well highlighted over the years. It was a calculated gamble based on the skills that the Haryana medium-pacer had displayed in the nets. It was also, says More, an instance of the unique Dhoni skill to match real-life situations with cricket.

'Often in life, the best person to go to in a desperate scenario is one who has nothing to lose. Joginder fit the bill perfectly, and all he wanted to hear was his captain say that he trusted him,' says More. Dhoni himself has often spoken about his captaincy as being based around gut-feel and using the experiences he's had in life. There are enough instances of those to fill up another book. How about the cheeky tactics he suggests to bowlers like untying and tying their shoelaces in the last over of an innings, especially in a run chase, to play with the batsman's mind and ruin their momentum.

'He has more confidence in his decisions than most of us normal people. All decisions he takes himself, and has had nobody to blame if they haven't worked out. He's never scared of taking a decision,' says Chittu.

It wasn't only on the field that Dhoni could pull a fast one on the opponent. He'd done it with the Pakistani team before that very final. On the eve of the match, Dhoni had spoken at length about the importance of Sehwag to the Indian team whenever they were playing Pakistan, even mentioning his great record against them.

Sehwag, it would be later revealed, was never in line to even play having pulled his hamstring a couple of days before the final. 'Getting Viru to just face a few balls in the nets was Mahi's googly. He said, "Why do we need to make it public or let the Pakistan team know that Sehwag isn't playing? Let them waste an hour worrying about Sehwag during their team meeting,'" says Chittu.

The first thing Dhoni does upon entering a dressing room for a practice session is have a cup or two of chai. Only then does he move on to cricketing activities. Meanwhile, within those walls, among his teammates, Dhoni is in the quest for banter.

When it came to communication within the dressing room, Dhoni also liked to maintain an honour code. That's why those who have shared the dressing room with him say that the one guaranteed way to get into the captain's bad books was by leaking any information. To my knowledge, there has been at least one player who has suffered Dhoni's wrath for having passed some on, and never been pardoned.

Dhoni demands a jovial atmosphere within the dressing room at all times. 'He has that kind of humour where he'll say one line with a straight face, and it'll hit you a few seconds later. He would already have started laughing by then,' says a former teammate.

Col Shankar who's spent a lot of time in Dhoni's hotel rooms adds that a good repartee is what gets his friend going the most. 'He loves it. Kedar Jadhav, in the present bunch, is great with his one-liners. And MS is so fond of them that he'll suddenly bring it up out of nowhere and say, "Sir, *yaad hai* (remember), I said this and Kedar *ne woh jawaab diya* (Kedar gave that answer)," and start laughing.'

A former teammate says anyone could mistake Dhoni to be a close friend simply because he is unassuming and accessible. However, only very few are allowed access beyond a point. It is almost a perfect mirror of how he is in the outside world. At most points in his career, Dhoni has had his own 'crew' or a bunch of teammates who he'll hang out with more than others. In some cases, because of him being captain, it has raised eyebrows and even led to ridicule whenever one among his crew is assumed to have been given a longer rope than someone not in it.

In later years, Dhoni has taken a different outlook—that of the senior citizen going out of his way to welcome the new entrants into the dressing room. This avatar of his really came to the fore in Zimbabwe in 2016 when he captained a team of second-stringers—players like Manish Pandey and Yuzvendra Chahal who have since cemented their place in the limited-overs' teams. While many in his position would have considered this a graveyard shift, he made the most of it, spending long hours in the nets with the youngsters. He also ensured that they spent time in his room, and ordered in food, while also playing PlayStation games with them and—winning.

Some say this is Dhoni's way of making up for not getting to meet new people most of the time and being cocooned in his room. The more you speak to those who've spent considerable time with him, you realize that trust and loyalty are not mere words for him, he truly believes in them.

'At times it could get funny. Muralitharan used to speak a lot in Tamil and Dhoni would say please only Hindi or English. Poor Murali then would only speak with those big eyes to the Tamilians in the team,' says a former CSK player.

You'll hear a lot of former cricketers nominate Dhoni as the one captain they would have loved to play under. Kiran More says that has mainly got to do with the fact that there was no real communication gap within the team under his reign.

There were, of course, a few times when there was a hitch in communication, but that was again handled well by Dhoni, says More, adding that he has always been transparent about whether certain players fit in the scheme of things or not. The writing, he says, was always on the wall and not in the air. 'He lets the team know what he thinks when they let him down. He backs them when they are down, but when they win, he's not there.'

Most of Dhoni's strong convictions about his relationships and how he handles them within the cricketing sphere can be traced back to certain incidents. His pet peeve over confidential information from selection meetings being leaked out came to a head in 2008, his first year of captaincy, when a newspaper report claimed that he'd got into a 'heated exchange' with the selectors over left-arm pacer R.P. Singh being dropped in favour of Irfan Pathan. The article had even gone on to claim that 'he (Dhoni) would quit if he didn't have his way'. This was during the one-day series against England at home. A clearly upset Dhoni addressed the media prior to the fourth ODI in Bangalore and though he never quite admitted to there being differences with the selection committee, he did express his 'disgust' over such reports and the issues that they could potentially cause between the players.

'In a scenario like this, you have to get in touch with both R.P. Singh and Irfan Pathan and ensure that there are no differences. RP shouldn't feel that I'm going out of the way in supporting him, nor should Irfan feel unwanted,' he'd said. He'd then emphasized his view that the confidentiality between the captain and the selectors should be respected at all times. 'I don't know from where the reports came from. What happens inside while the selectors and the captains are there, if it comes out, it's disgusting, it's disrespecting. I think if they are supposed to come out, it's better (that) we have live television in the room there. What happens, nobody should know apart from the eight guys who are sitting down,' Dhoni had insisted.

But when it came to the media, both communication and trust weren't his greatest traits. For someone who has spent half his life endorsing and promoting cell-phone networks, Dhoni has always remained 'out of coverage area' as far as journalists are concerned.

Dhoni's relationship with the media hit an all-time low after India's embarrassing exit from the 2007 World Cup, when the team was back home within the first ten days of the lengthy tournament.

Dhoni spent a few days in Delhi and upon returning to Ranchi, would lock himself up in Chittu's house most part of the day and not meet anyone. Since everyone in Ranchi knew that a black Scorpio parked in front of Chittu's house can mean only one thing, Dhoni would insist on the door being bolted and locked from the outside to ward off anyone trying to sneak up on him.

So, Chittu makes quite a revelation when he says that there was a time when Dhoni was close to the local journalists. 'It was in my house where he would often call them over after each of his early cricketing feats, and I have served chai to them myself. But the reactions after the 2007 World Cup and a few unsavoury comments changed everything. After winning the World T20, he didn't bother about them and came straight home from the airport,' Chittu says.

The Dhoni interview is the ultimate El Dorado for an Indian cricket journalist, simply for the reason that it hasn't happened for nearly a decade. And those who were fortunate enough to have sat him down for an on-the-record chat before he became captain recall a candid, polite and punctual young man. In the years since, the proclamation 'I interviewed Dhoni once' has become a sure-shot way to attract attention in press boxes and press clubs around the country.

Back then, they say, if Dhoni said he'd give you an interview, you could rest assured he would. Not much has changed now, except that when Dhoni says he won't give you an interview, you can rest assured he never will.

A senior journalist recalls how reluctant Dhoni was to address the media upon being named the ODI captain following the 2007 series in England. It was only after the coaxing of a few old hands that he agreed. 'I said, "*Bolo din mein suraj hota hai, raat ko chand hota hai.* (Just say that during the day, there is sun, and at night, there's moon.) Say anything, but at least say a few words." "*Theek hai.*"(All right.)," he said. However, he added that he doesn't like this media exposure.'

And Dhoni has stayed true to his word. His lengthy interview to Mark Nicholas a few years ago in England did cause considerable heartburn back home. But he's more or less been impartial about politely turning down interview requests, even last year to Sky Sports after he was invited specially to Lord's for a charity match.

He isn't the first superstar cricketer in the country to build a wall around himself. But it was different with Dhoni. Tendulkar had that aura of greatness about him. You were convinced that you could see and maybe even feel that bulwark around him. With Dhoni it was more a line. It was often invisible, but somehow you knew it couldn't be crossed.

I believe that to a certain extent, Dhoni got the cricket media to approach the team differently. The captains who had come before him were never so unapproachable. It wasn't quite like how things were in the 1980s and '90s when journalists and cricketers, including the captain, enjoyed freewheeling relationships. But the likes of Ganguly, Dravid and Tendulkar didn't always keep journalists at arm's length like Dhoni would.

Ganguly, of course, had his media entourage. Even the likes of Dravid, Tendulkar and Kumble never seemed so cut off from the media as Dhoni. Perhaps as a result, or maybe it's a coincidence, the Indian dressing room also seemed selectively porous back then. That changed with Dhoni's arrival.

His unflappable view that what's said in the dressing room should stay there meant that journalists had to be particularly imaginative to find an opening. They started tapping into other sources available in the dressing room, for they had to. In his own way, and I'm guessing he had no intention of doing so, he knocked the Indian cricket media out of their comfort zone. It wasn't always easy, like when he suddenly retired from Test cricket, in Melbourne. The team hotel went into a lockdown, with the liaison officer posted in the lobby to identify and smoke out Indian journalists who would inevitably try to make their way in to catch a whiff of how Dhoni's shock decision had panned out. The rest of the night was spent fighting the chilly and stiff Yarra River breeze.

I wonder how many of my colleagues have wished like me that Dhoni's press conferences were held with him behind the stump mic rather than on a podium. Our jobs would have been so much easier. By the way, former cricketer V.B. Chandrasekhar says that most of Dhoni's non-stop advice to the spinners is in a similar tone to the one he prefers hearing suggestions in. It's never 'upar daal (pitch it up), chota daal (pitch it short) or dheere daal' (bowl slowly). It's always 'upar daal sakte hai . . . dheere daal sakte hai' (you could pitch it up . . . you could bowl slowly), as if they are polite recommendations.

A number of his wisecracks from press conferences are recounted over and over. They offer a peek into his mind. A lot of journalists take a Dhoni press briefing to be a crash course on reductio ad absurdum. My favourite Dhoni press conferences came overseas, on those rare tours where the room wasn't brimming with Indian faces. Here he would be candid, honest and, at times, amusing. I'll never forget his dig at Ishant Sharma after winning the tri-series in Port of Spain in 2013 with a last-over six. Asked about a slight mix-up in the running, he quipped, 'I had just told him one ball before that if it is an easy single, we will take it, but then fast bowlers run. The fast bowler is too tall. There is much distance between the brain and the receptors.' Back in India, he always seemed more reluctant.

Indian captains have always made for interesting viewing at press conferences. Legend has it that Azharuddin would be so relaxed that during one such meet he was trimming his toenails while answering the questions. A Dravid press conference would often be a class on diplomacy. But he did seem happier to answer questions that sounded intelligent to him. With Sachin Tendulkar, you almost immediately knew what he thought of your question. His eyes said it all.

Dhoni always gives you the feeling that he could have been doing something a lot more fun than telling you about his team composition. Absurd questions would amuse him. I remember one before a Kochi ODI against Australia in 2010, which witnessed so much rain that the team never even had to leave the hotel. After providing Dhoni with details of exactly how far the hotel was—in kilometres—from the stadium, airport and the market, the journalist wanted to know what the captain had been up to in those three rain-washed days. Dhoni actually complimented him for his left-field question and spoke about how he'd gotten bored of being asked about team combinations and pitch conditions. And controversial topics would generally set off his penchant for analogies.

As captain, he didn't always shy away or cower from facing the press. But there were times he could have come forward and perhaps provided a clearer appraisal of some of his and the team's decisions. Like why they didn't go for the run chase during the third Test of the 2011 tour in Dominica despite having wickets in hand. It was instead new coach Duncan Fletcher who was left to face the fire.

There was that infamous press meet before the team's departure for the Champions Trophy in 2013 when he simply smiled when facing volleys about the spot-fixing scandal. It was one of those moments when you thought Dhoni perhaps would have done himself less harm by just saying, 'I won't answer questions regarding the issue' rather than just sit there with a strange grin on his face. As a journalist, you couldn't help but feel like you were being mocked.

Dhoni, though, would make it a point to be there whenever the team lost. Kohli has started doing the same these days. This wasn't always the case in the past. Unlike teams like England, Australia and South Africa, the Indian media manager doesn't quite make the final call on who attends the press conferences. It's mostly the captain's call, or on rare occasions, it's left to the coach. Considering India has lost a lot away from home, Dhoni has put himself out there on a fair few occasions. Once even showing up in Harare after India lost a T20 after he fell short of finishing the game in the last over. I remember telling him before the media conference that the pressure, if anything, was more on me—considering there were just two journalists from India covering the tour, while there were a billion or so waiting back home to hear how I put Dhoni on the spot following this upset. He seemed rather amused by that prospect.

'*Ice bhi pigal jaayega, lekin Dhoni nahi.* (Ice melts, but not Dhoni.),' Harbhajan had once famously said about his former captain. But even the famed Dhoni calm started eroding towards the end of his Indian captaincy tenure; constant queries about his future in the game would be met with stinging ripostes. There was also the time when he called an Australian journalist for a tête-à- tête after India were knocked out of the 2016 World T20. Sam Ferris, who works for cricket.com.au, had asked Dhoni how long he would continue to play limited-overs cricket, to which the then Indian captain invited the Australian to join him on the podium. In a bizarre turn of events, Dhoni turned inquisitor and grilled Ferris with queries like 'Do you want me to retire?' and 'Do you think I'm unfit, looking at me running?' He also said that he'd hoped it would be an Indian journalist who would ask him about his future. 'You fired the wrong ammunition at the wrong time,' Dhoni told Ferris in front of a packed room located underground at the Wankhede. The Aussie would then write a piece for his website about how a 'fairly routine question for a 34-year-old skipper just eliminated from the World T20' turned him into 'an unwitting media spectacle'.[*]

Maybe Dhoni was just trying to be funny. But the humour didn't come across tastefully. It left a bitter taste in the mouth for many in the Indian media. 'If you keep poking at the same wound, I will react. I am human too. Or are you saying I can't even react like a human any more?' he would tell a senior journalist when asked about this never-before-seen temper.

There was another incident during that same tournament when a journalist asked Dhoni whether the narrow win over Bangladesh was satisfactory enough considering his team needed to win with a bigger margin to improve their net run rate. 'Listen to me. Hearing you, your tone and your question, it's clear that you aren't happy that India has won. And when talking about a cricket match, there's no script. It's not about the script,' he'd said. 'You have to analyse that after losing the toss, what was the reason that we couldn't make many runs on that wicket? If you aren't analysing these things sitting outside, then you shouldn't ask this question.'

It was the kind of anger you rarely saw from Dhoni.

***

[*] Sam Ferris, 'My Sit-down Chat with India Skipper MS Dhoni', Cricket.com.au, 1 April 2016, https://www.cricket.com.au/news/feature/ms-dhoni-samuel-ferris-retirement-question-press-conference-world-t20-west-indies-semi-final/2016-04-01.

The happiest I ever saw Dhoni at a press conference was arguably his last as an active player. He'd stepped down from the captaincy a few days earlier. And when asked what he wouldn't miss much, he, not surprisingly, mentioned press conferences. 'We don't need press conference every day. I always felt, there is too much exposure.' He was pretty much repeating what he'd said the day he took over as captain a decade earlier.

8

Pythagoras behind the Stumps

It was a mundane event during the 2017 IPL final in Hyderabad. Rising Pune Supergiant skipper Steve Smith had thrown a ball in from the boundary and Dhoni had collected it behind the stumps. At that point, the wicketkeeper had provided his old coach Banerjee with a moment of nostalgia probably without even realizing it.

'*Hum usko pakad liya.* (I noticed it.) The ball came in and at the last minute, his hands went into that *machli-ka-mooh* (fish-mouth) position. It was just like old times,' the coach says, giggling. It's basically what old-school coaches and cricket prudes consider a loutish way of catching a ball. It's when you position your hands one above the other—rather than side by side like the manual recommends—and cup them eventually like a trapdoor shutting. Being a Bengali, it was only natural that Banerjee brought in a machli reference. And just for the record, Dhoni isn't into seafood.

'I used to constantly be on his case to change it (his catching technique). Whenever I was watching, he would do it properly. The moment my head turned away or I was talking to someone, machli ka mooh would start again,' says Banerjee, shaking his head.

In gully cricket, at least in urban India, how you catch a ball can often be the deciding factor between whether you are an *asli* (real) cricketer or a *nakli* (fake) one. It's not been too different for Dhoni on the international circuit. Purists have always turned their nose up at his wicketkeeping technique only because it is different, slightly ungainly even. But how do you pick on someone who sits third on the list of all-time highest dismissals among wicketkeepers across formats? Not to forget the man who's stumped more batsmen than anyone else in history. Former Australian opener Michael Slater called him 'the fastest gloves in the west'.

'People talk about his technique a lot and say that it's bad. I never bought that. He's a street-smart wicketkeeper. And if at the right time you don't take the bails off, what's the point of having a perfect technique? MS has redefined stumpings,' says Kiran More, not a slouch himself behind the stumps.

Dhoni, if anything, has redefined the right time to take the bails off. He does it three frames quicker than his counterparts. That is two frames quicker than what the batsman has to get his foot back in the crease, which is nigh impossible. And it's no overstatement to say that he almost seems to stop time itself while executing one of his trademark stumpings.

'He's the standard bearer when it comes to stumpings. We're all trying to get to at least 50–60 per cent of the speed at which he whips the bails off,' Dinesh Karthik had told me while I was working on a piece trying to decipher the Dhoni way of wicketkeeping some two years ago.[*]

Someone who was scoffed at for not heeding the wicketkeeping manual, seems to now be one step ahead of it. He's certainly quite a few steps ahead of the poor batsman. That front popping crease must feel like a landmine marking for a batsman when he has Dhoni lurking behind him. He's always just one wrong step on the wrong side of the crease away from disaster. This is white-line fever of a totally new kind, all thanks to Dhoni. It is cricket's own *lakshman rekha*.

The MMA-type speed he generates comes from a variety of factors. But it's mainly to do with his singular style of collecting the ball behind the stumps. No, we're not talking about machli ka mooh here. That's only when the coach isn't looking or when Dhoni is feeling nostalgic.

Dhoni 'uses force to absorb force' with his hands. Most keepers do what other mortals do, which is, push their hands back to cushion the blow after catching the ball. That's how they absorb the force. That's how they produce the 'give' to ensure the ball doesn't pop out. Dhoni, though, is pushing forward, as in, generating 'give' in the direction from which the ball is coming.

---

[*] Bharat Sundaresan, 'Latest from MS Dhoni: Pythagoras in Gloves', *Indian Express*, 15 May 2016, http://indianexpress.com/article/sports/cricket/ms-dhonis-pythagoras-in-gloves-ipl-2016-rising-pune-supergiants-2801036/.

It's like when you are getting off a train and the nearest exit on the platform is behind you. While all others would step out in the direction in which the train's moving, stop their momentum and then turn around, Dhoni, you imagine, wouldn't have to worry about the tiny detour. He could just as well jump straight out against the momentum of the train, and look as unperturbed as ever while doing so.

In fact, this analogy perhaps stands true for his running between the wickets too. Never will you see Dhoni over-running, as in he puts on the brakes with his running exactly when he needs to with relation to the crease. It means that he never wastes even an extra millisecond in turning around for the second or third run, and that makes him one of the best runners in the world. Then there's the natural speed across the 22 yards that's hardly diminished even now in his late thirties. Dhoni still takes great pride in being the fastest in the Indian dressing room in short-distance running. 'The day there's someone who's faster than me in a 50-metre sprint, I'll know it's time to go,' he's known to tell teammates in jest.

The unbelievable thing is that he doesn't push forward with hard hands either, which would get the ball to pop out more often than not. The wrists remain supple enough to soak in all the force. And we're not always talking spinners here either. Dhoni has even stood up to the likes of Irfan Pathan at his peak and pulled off stumpings.

It's just another example of his unbelievable natural strength. Those forearms are the reason he generates such power with the helicopter shot. They are also responsible for why he's been able to rewrite the physics of wicketkeeping.

His teammates don't need an illustration of their former captain's brute strength. But he doesn't mind reminding them of it on occasions. Once, towards the end of a practice session, the Indian players, led by Virat Kohli, decided to have a competition. The object was to stand beyond the boundary ropes and see how far they could underarm a ball. Dhoni had just finished his nets session and was packing his gear. But as he saw the others go through with it, he got tempted. It was, of course, a unique opportunity for Dhoni to do something he rarely gets to do—throw the ball from the outfield to the centre. It took him a single turn to be declared winner. His underarm flick saw the ball land one bounce on the pitch. Game over.

'His stumpings turned heads even back then. In that same school final where he scored all those runs, what I remember most is him getting five stumpings. I told him he's taken five wickets. He stood up to everyone back then, fast bowlers, spinners, everyone,' says coach Banerjee.

Kiran More, though, believes Dhoni's self-taught technique of collecting the ball often overshadows the skill that actually deserves the limelight—his positioning. The former selector believes that his positioning gives him the extra two seconds and a 90 per cent strike rate as a stumper. He likens it to how Tendulkar could read the length of the ball from the time the bowler released it.

'When your positioning is so good, you will make it look that easy, especially for someone with such soft hands as MS. If you're not in position, you have to move your hands that extra bit more and you lose time. It's like batting. If you're in line with the ball, you'll connect with it every time. You'll never see MS being late to a ball. He's already there. That's because he knows where the ball or the throw from the boundary is going to come and where he needs to stand. It reduces his reaction time,' he explains, adding that the only other keeper he has seen being as quick was England's Bob Taylor.

In addition to the strength, the technique and the positioning, Dhoni's eye for detail is what makes him such an unforgiving judge, jury and executioner from behind the stumps. It is, in Col Shankar's opinion, another one of his friend's fauji traits.

Officers and soldiers are both made to develop through repeated drills the ability to spot the slightest thing that's amiss. It could often be the difference between winning or losing a battle. 'Somebody will do the drill and he'll make some intentional mistakes where you're expected to pick them out. Some will be very evident but most will be subtle and be hidden by a larger action. It's basically done so that we are always aware when things are even slightly out of place, especially while on patrol,' Shankar says.

Dhoni, he says, is naturally gifted with that skill. Anything that's not routine always catches his eye. It's the reason why he's so spot-on with his observations from behind the stumps about a batsman's movements or intentions. How often have we heard spinner after spinner attribute a chunk of his success to the advice that comes from Dhoni?

Kuldeep Yadav, India's latest chinaman sensation, and Yuzvendra Chahal never failed to mention Dhoni's contribution to their unprecedented, if not prodigious, success during the one-day leg of India's tour to South Africa in early 2018. 'As a spinner, he (Dhoni) does 50 per cent of your work because he has played so much cricket; he reads the batsmen easily,' Yadav had said after his maiden outing on South African soil, saying how Dhoni had asked him to 'bowl as he was bowling' after he'd been confused about the strong wind and the resultant drift on the ball at Durban. 'From behind the stumps, Mahi-bhai always keeps advising you. He knows what the batsman is going to try. It makes it easier for us,' Chahal had said after snaring seven wickets in the first two matches of that series.

'I'm able to see how a batsman stands and how he reacts, and tell the bowler this is what he's going to do. It could be that he's moved an inch this side or that side or something even subtler,' he'd once explained to the colonel. There was the stumping of Bangladesh's Sabbir Rahman in the 2016 World T20 tournament. Not only was it a quick take down the leg-side, but Dhoni timed the removing of the bails at the precise moment that Sabbir raised his foot.

This singular Dhoni trait can also be a thorn in the side for those close to him. Ask the colonel. Last year, he released one of his many caricature books—he collects caricatures which generally focus on his sporting idols—this one entirely about the players in the Pune franchise. Dhoni's first reaction was, '*Bahut bhadiya hai*, sir. (Very good, sir.)' He then flicked through the pages once. Within a second, he'd spotted the one factual mistake in the book.

'He didn't even turn many pages. One flick, and he tells me that Jaskaran Singh, the Jharkhand seam bowler, is a left-armer but the cartoon shows him as a right-armer,' Shankar recalls.

Another time when Dhoni was shown a caricature someone had made of him, he told the colonel almost immediately, '*Isme toh mere daant hai.* (I have teeth here.)' 'He has a couple of molars missing, but the caricature hadn't detailed that fact. And he caught it with one look; that's his eye for detail. It happens all the time. He'll keep saying, "*Sir, aapne woh galat kiya, woh wahan nahi hona chahiye tha.* (Sir, you did it wrong; it shouldn't be there.) It's a constant flow,' the colonel adds.

Like with that Sabbir stumping, the keenness to observe has helped Dhoni challenge the old adage that good wicketkeeping is one that you don't notice during a day's play. That's what they say about good drummers too. With Dhoni, you're always expecting him to create something out of nothing. Has there been any other wicketkeeper who's featured as much as he has in highlights packages simply for his glove work?

'People get excited about how a keeper does on a turning track, but I've never understood the fuss. On that kind of a pitch, the keeper is always the hero. The attention is on him anyway. It's on a flat track, where the ball comes to you once every half hour, and you still are able to be a hero that makes you a special wicketkeeper, like MS does so often,' says More.

In the 2016 edition of the IPL, he created not just a new trend but a new position for a wicketkeeper. It was a physical demonstration of inscrutable innovation. That bizarre-looking concoction he'd stewed by lifting his right leg at a right angle and parallel to the ground to thwart a batsman's late-cut attempts. I'd called him cricket's Pythagoras at that point and even described his manoeuvre using the primordial theorem to back the coinage. Dhoni's Pythagoras move first appeared during Rising Pune Supergiant's outing against Kings XI Punjab on 17 April 2016.

'He ensures that his gloves remain in their original place. For, by creating the angle that he does with his extended foot, Dhoni does manage to double his reach while having both his hands and legs in perfect positions to stop the ball.' That's how I'd described it.

When Dhoni isn't creating scenarios, he's using his presence of mind to manipulate or influence them. The stumping of David Warner during the league encounter against Australia at the 2016 World T20 tourney in Mohali was one such example. He'd softened his left hand at the last moment to ensure that the ball didn't bounce out but rather bounced off it and landed right back in the gloves for him to pull the stumping off. There was also that last-over runout in a World T20 against Bangladesh where he ran in from behind the stumps, not to speak of the dozens and hundreds of those during his career.

They don't always have to result in a dismissal. During a tense finish to a Mumbai vs Pune IPL league match at the Wankhede stadium, Dan Christian had taken an extremely low catch on the boundary and rolled the ball back in. The entire Pune team naturally rushed towards the Australian all-rounder in delight. The catch meant that Pune were now favourites to win the contest. All except Dhoni. He instead focused on the stray ball and ran across to his left to collect it. It was a low catch, and he knew that camera angles could easily cast doubts over the legality of the catch, or at least create illusionary doubts. So, why risk that and give away an overthrow four. That's how Dhoni's brain works. It never stops. It's always on the ball. The conclusion of the match is a dramatic one. A controversial wide call leads to a stoppage in play as the Mumbai Indians' skipper Rohit Sharma marches up to umpire S. Ravi for what would turn out to be a clarification regarding the wide rule. Dhoni remains unmoved with his hands behind his back. Next ball, Rohit is out caught by bowler Jaidev Unadkat off a top-edged skier. In the process, Unadkat's head hits the hard square and he is writhing in pain. The entire team rushes to see if he's okay. Dhoni, instead, walks to umpire Ravi and seeks clarification on whether Rohit and Harbhajan Singh had crossed each other when the catch was being taken. That would mean Harbhajan would be on strike for the next delivery. The Dhoni brain never stops whirring. It's always, always on the ball.

V.B. Chandrasekhar says it's the ability to read the pulse of a batsman from behind the stumps that has made Dhoni such a successful wicketkeeper and an intuitive captain in limited-overs cricket. He brings up the case of the fielder whom he'd placed in the 2010 IPL final to get rid of Kieron Pollard—right behind the bowler.

'He seems to feel the vibrations from a batsman and tell where he's likely to hit the ball. He's also got an unbelievable sense of angles on a cricket field, like that fielder for Pollard proves,' says Chandrasekhar.

It's perhaps the fact that batsmen aren't as anxious to score or play more shots in the longer format that didn't work in Dhoni's favour as a Test captain. Unlike in ODIs and T20s, he rarely seemed to be a step ahead of the game. In most cases, as a Test captain, he was playing catch-up. And he never seemed at his best doing that. It must be said that he didn't always have the kind of bowling attack required to generate pressure on the opposition on away tours.

Dhoni, the Test wicketkeeper, had a few hiccups too. It generally came away from home when he would often not go for a catch when the ball flew between him and the slips. There were also times in England, especially during the 2011 tour, where he had problems with the ball moving a lot after passing the batsman. He wasn't the first foreign keeper to fall victim to this quirk in English conditions. Kiran More recalls how Dhoni had called him to his room to discuss the issue.

'We spoke about hand positions and leg positions. He's a smart learner and he understands even the minute points. It doesn't need to be hands-on coaching with him. You discuss one point with him and he'll immediately pick it up and work with it,' says More. It's a quality that M.P. Singh, who was Dhoni's coach at the national stadium in Delhi and played a huge role in his development as a wicketkeeper, too raves about. Dhoni, to date, never fails to touch Singh's feet whenever they meet.

'If someone says something cannot be done, then Mahi will make sure that he disproves them by overcoming that challenge. And you get to see this tendency even while he is practising in the nets,' Singh says.

Dhoni, though, for no fault of his, might be responsible for a lot of young wicketkeepers in the country not practising their art enough. R. Sridhar, India's fielding coach, once said that he'd seen Dhoni practise his keeping thrice in the two years he'd been with the national team. Dhoni has got a similar theory about T20 cricket and not fussing too much over it during practice. It's almost like he believes that they know enough cricket to just go out there and play their game and not bother about overdoing the practice.

More says it's a trend that he has seen catching on among the younger wicketkeepers and how he ends up having to give them the same lecture about what works for Dhoni will never work for anyone who's not Dhoni. 'I've seen Sunil Gavaskar not practising much, keep leaving balls, get bowled three to ten times, and next day, hit the ball as sweetly as ever in the match. But he was special like Dhoni. MS too does his own drills. He plays badminton for his eyesight, for example,' says More.

He also agrees with my theory that every Dhoni wicketkeeping video should come necessarily with a WWE-style disclaimer. Whether it's him showcasing the Nataraja pose or catching the ball like he's catching fish, the world needs to be forewarned to not 'try a Dhoni at home, school, work or while getting off the train'.

9

Thala

It is a plain No. 7 yellow jersey with nothing else but Thala written on it. 'Nuff said. There is no CSK logo. There is no India Cements logo. They're not required. Dhoni has made his point. CSK are back. And so is their Thala.

It is 15 July 2017, the day after CSK's two-year suspension has ceased. The two-time official champions are now part of the IPL family again. Dhoni has just returned from a lengthy tour, which started in England for the Champions Trophy and was followed by a three-week dash around the Caribbean. And here he is posing in front of his home with pet dog Sam saluting his Thala for good measure in the background.

There was a lot of speculation in the media about how CSK would announce their return. Would it be an elaborate ad campaign? Maybe a bunch of catchy WWE-style vignettes with some whistles thrown in there? Sure, the two-time champions who've always boasted of the most zealous fan following in the IPL wouldn't make a comeback without any fanfare. Then, Dhoni does just that. The message is subtle and all-encompassing at the same time. And they don't have to do anything else.

But if you thought it was a well-planned and executed master stroke from the CSK management, then think again. For, on July 15, while Dhoni's Thala picture was going viral, S. Chockalingam and his team were sitting in shock at their offices in Chennai. Chockalingam, or Chocka, is the creative director at OPN Advertising, which has handled CSK's ad and social media campaigns since the franchise's inception.

'He did it by himself totally. None of us had anything to do with it. It was a total surprise to us when we saw his Instagram post,' says Chocka.

Thala is simply Tamil for head. And unless you're from Chennai, there's no other significance to it. In Chennai, it's a title. It's not to be confused with *Thalaiva*, which is, of course, Rajinikanth. Even if he might walk the streets like an ordinary man, Rajinikanth is a demigod who, simply put, is above everyone and everything else—if you are prone to hyperbole, like most of the great man's fans. In a city so obsessed with cinema, his is a status that is unattainable. To the extent that I've never heard Thalaiva being used lightly, even amongst a bunch of friends. Unlike how Thala is, and frequently so. Thala is someone you can relate to.

Perhaps it's got to do with the man who holds that title, Ajith, a romantic hero turned action star. He is unlike other movie heroes in the south. While he does enjoy a cult following, Ajith doesn't carry an aura or a halo. Despite playing superhero on the screen routinely, off it his greatest attribute is how he has never let his superstardom take over his life. He's somehow escaped from becoming larger than life, much like Dhoni has. So Thala was a perfect fit for Chennai's latest superstar, and, of course, the fact that he was CSK captain. They share more in common too.

Dhoni loves bikes. Ajith loves cars. When Dhoni's not playing, he's taking his beloved bikes for a ride around Ranchi. Ajith is a race car driver and competes around the world.

'We called him Thala for the first time in the Whistle Podu version in 2010. We were apprehensive in the beginning about whether it'll be accepted, considering how big Ajith is. But people accepted Dhoni readily as their Thala, and though it took him a while, he is now very aware of the significance of being one,' says Chocka.

CSK is unlike the nearly hundred other brands and products that Dhoni has endorsed as the ultimate pan-Indian pin-up boy of the advertising industry over the last ten years. Some might argue it's not even in the same bracket as a pure brand. But think of all the brands that Dhoni has been an ambassador for and still none has become as synonymous with him as CSK.

And you can't help but agree with V.B. Chandrasekhar when he says, 'In Chennai when they see Dhoni's face, they see a lion, and when they see a lion's face, they see Dhoni.' Dramatic indeed, almost like a Thalaiva movie scene.

We will touch upon the Dhoni–Chennai love affair in the next chapter. But I want to probe a little further here into what really makes this unlikely twain meet. Straightaway, I realize it's not the usual case of opposites attracting. The more I ask, the more I realize that this aspect of Dhoni's life is less enigmatic and more meant-to-be.

Chocka believes that while 'small town boy making it big' narratives strike a chord in most places around the country, nowhere else are they as much an inherent fibre of mainstream cinema as in Chennai.

'Oh, at one point of time he was like us and now he's right up there where we can only dream of being. That immediately brought them closer to him. And the fact that he's remained understated like most of our stars, including Rajinikanth, while not in film, added authenticity and more appeal to him,' says Chocka.

Chandrasekhar recalls having told Dhoni after seeing him lift his dhoti and dance with Prabhu Deva in a bike ad that he would have to do better since 'we are the land of Rajinikanth'. 'I think I will do as well as him (as an actor),' Dhoni had replied in jest. Like Rajinikanth though, who shows up at all public events looking his age and without any frills, Dhoni can rarely, if ever, be spotted wearing shades inside an airport terminal, which for some reason is considered a professional hazard by most celebrities.

Col Shankar, meanwhile, feels that it's the lack of showiness among even the rich and wealthy in Chennai—in terms of the modesty in attire—that has drawn Dhoni towards his adopted home.

'Sir, pata nahi tha itna bada aadmi hai woh, ghar gaye tabhi pata chala. Gaadi khadi thi. Woh toh chappal aur dhoti pehenke aa jaata hai, sir. (Sir, I didn't know he was such a big man. Only after going to his house did I realize. There was a vehicle parked there. He used to come wearing dhoti and chappals, sir.),' Dhoni would often reveal his bemusement to the colonel.

Dhoni and Chennai could possibly have more cricket-related reasons for their successful courtship. While Chennai—or Madras, as it was called once—has always been counted among the powerhouses of Indian cricket, locals there have never really had a homegrown icon player. Unlike Mumbai, Delhi, Bengaluru, Kolkata, Hyderabad or even Chandigarh for that matter, they've never boasted of that one player who has given them bragging rights for a period of time.

R. Ashwin comes the closest. He's already the most capped Test cricketer from the state alongside S. Venkataraghavan. And nobody from Tamil Nadu has even got close to Kris Srikkanth's 146 ODIs, the last of which came twenty-five years ago. This was true in 2008 as well, when most other big cities with a 'cricket culture' had their own 'icon' player to lead their respective franchises. Chennai went looking for one. So when Dhoni came along, they just swooped in and made him their own.

Chennai's claim to have the most 'knowledgeable cricket crowd' in the country has always invoked sniggers from most quarters. But it is true that no other venue has quite witnessed genuine appreciation for the opposition like Chepauk has over the years. Don't forget, they even gave the Pakistani team a standing ovation—a blasphemous act for many venues around India you'd think. 'They (the Chepauk spectators) are overall docile and not so rooted to the feeling of "only we can win",' says Chandrasekhar.

He also believes that they only learnt to be partisan after Dhoni's arrival. He recalls a match from IPL III where CSK chased down a biggish total against Kings XI Punjab. The video of that finish is worth watching. Dhoni hit Irfan Pathan for 16 runs in the final over, sealing it off with a six—his customary finishing manoeuvre of clubbing the ball over deep mid-wicket. What happened next has always left me intrigued. For one night alone, Dhoni celebrated like it mattered. It started with him shouting out what seemed like an expletive before he quickly lowered his head and continued muttering. He then delivered an upper-cut to himself with his visor taking the brunt. I've always wondered whether the punch was just a continuation of that adrenaline discharge or whether he was remonstrating himself for having been demonstrative. He's never come close to looking as pumped as he did that night in Dharamsala. The Dalai Lama was in attendance for that game. Chandrasekhar believes that the passion to win which their captain exuded so brazenly despite being someone who rarely indulges in any show of emotion, was what has changed the Chennai crowds and made them even more desperate for their team to win.

'They don't want to win . . . they desperately want to win. He didn't have to do much. He just had to be himself,' says Chandrasekhar. Just like he had to only get himself in front of a camera to tell the CSK universe to whistle for their Thala all over again.

The Whistle Podu campaign, for all its raging popularity, didn't come about from some great urge to create a phenomenon. It was more out of the fear of missing out. OPN Advertising is an interesting company. They still don't have an official website despite having a client of CSK's worth. But they can be forgiven. They're still probably the only company in India that has a canine worker on board—Goofy, who has his own corner seat and business card, and was featured by the BBC, no less.* And they've been at the forefront of turning CSK into a rather chic outfit with smart and snappy ad campaigns and concepts.

Back in 2009, when the IPL was shifted to South Africa, Chocka—who is one of the partners at OPN—was told to pack his bags and go to cheer CSK. As luxurious an offer as it was, he wasn't chuffed. Fortunately, Hayden, Suresh Raina and Parthiv Patel were to spend a couple of days practising at Chepauk before flying out, and Chocka jumped at the opportunity. He was given half-hour windows to shoot whatever he chose with them. The challenge, as he reveals, was to come up with a way to engage with the fans when the team was away.

'There was no point asking them to cheer for CSK. They'd do that anyway. So, we decided to show them how to cheer. And whistle was the obvious thing. On the first day, first show of any superstar movie in Chennai you'll hear only whistles. Whistle Podu was born,' says Chocka.

---

* Geeta Pandey, 'Meet One Indian Ad Firm's "Top Dog"', BBC, 19 August 2016, http://www.bbc.com/news/world-asia-india-37092728.

Dhoni wasn't part of the video—which went viral and was soon being sought after by the IPL's official broadcasters—in 2009. But he was more than happy to be included when Chocka wrote to him a year later. Dhoni's part was to be shot in the Chepauk dressing room after he was done with a practice session. Chocka was told he'd have five minutes. And five minutes was all it took. Dhoni came, said his line, 'Chennai Super Kings *ku* whistle podu', whistled in his own way and left. All in one take.

This wasn't the first time Chocka had shot with Dhoni. He had done a few stills with him in 2008 for IPL I. And at that first meeting itself he'd learnt what to expect from a Dhoni shoot.

It starts with punctuality. Many a client or agency have been caught off guard by Dhoni landing up a few minutes before schedule, but never has he kept even one of them waiting. And once he's there, Chocka emphasizes, he's all yours. Some have even heard him say 'I am all yours'. But he's particular about the time he gives. With Dhoni, thirty minutes is thirty minutes, not a minute more, not a minute less. He's even known to set the stopwatch on his phone the moment he walks in. Chocka has been a witness to it. But like in life and on the cricket field, the principles that form the basis of Dhoni's life shine through even in the studio.

'He's extremely in the moment here too. He might give us only five minutes, but that entire five minutes he's with us. His mind is not anywhere else. He understands what we are trying to do and why we are doing it,' says Chocka. In that first meeting 10 years ago, he also learnt about another Dhoni quirk.

'That first shoot was just a few stills in a yellow jersey. He was very particular about the size and the fit of the jersey. He tried a few out before settling on one. He gave us thirty minutes and we were done by the 29th and he was happy.'

Prahlad Kakkar hasn't worked extensively with Dhoni but has done a few ads with him, including a few snappy ones for a pen company. The veteran ad guru counts him as one of the most cooperative and amenable celebrities he's worked with. He also remembers him as being someone who doesn't interfere much unless he has one of his ingenious ideas to share.

'He's a natural. You ask him to do something and he'll do it in his own way. You ask him to do something, *aisa kar, waise kar* (do it this way, that way), he'll turn around and say, "*Mein actor nahi hoon. Mein aise hi karoonga.* (I am not an actor. I'll do it this way only.),"' Kakkar tells me.

I hear the 'not an actor' reference from one of Dhoni's close aides too, with regard to how he views endorsements. While he's aware of his brand value—which has made him a fixture in Forbes' richest sportspersons list for a number of years—he remains an eternal realist about its longevity or the lack of it.

'Brand endorsements *sab jhoot hai.* (Brand endorsements are all lies.) If I do this, I will get that, nothing like that exists. Tendulkar-paaji has told me one thing. You can improve every day as a cricketer. But by acting, I can't become Amitabh Bachchan. I need to concentrate on what builds my brand, and that's my cricket,' he's known to have told an aide once.

Now, Chocka doesn't say Dhoni is ever going to give Bachchan a run for his money, not now and not twenty years later either. But he insists that Dhoni rarely needs more than a single take to pull off whatever acting challenges get thrown at him. He brings up a digital shoot they did for a global oil company, which also happens to be his client, with Ajinkya Rahane and Faf du Plessis in the mix. Dhoni and his teammates were shown various scenarios from a match and asked to react as naturally as possible to the camera.

'Oh my god, he was brilliant,' Chocka exclaims, before adding, 'I got Dhoni to react to things like somebody hitting a six, somebody missing a ball and his reactions were so spontaneous and brilliant. After seeing one clip, he said, "Arré, but I would never show any reaction to this on the field." But when I insisted, he said, "Okay, let me have some fun with it." He was superb.'

And for a change, Dhoni apparently wasn't ready to leave once his time was up. He wanted to stay back and see how Rahane was going to cope with the test. 'With Jinks (Rahane), most of the reactions were the same, and Dhoni was rolling on the floor literally. I have never seen him laugh so much. I had never seen that side of him,' says Chocka. This was perhaps Dhoni's 'childlike' sense of humour which Matthew Hayden had told Gaurav Kapoor about on his show, *Breakfast with Champions*. 'He has got that cheeky humour you probably do not see, but it's all those silly things. He is not going to do all that stand-up comedy act. He is very childlike. He has retained his sense of passion from when he was 7. I love that about his personality,' he tells Kapoor on the show where the actor-turned-IPL host gets cricketers to open up and show a side of them that rarely or never surfaces anywhere else in the public sphere.

There are, in fact, a number of videos, generally to do with photo shoots, where Dhoni is seen getting stuck into a young cricketer for his acting or overacting, like he does these days with Hardik Pandya.

It's not just the ease with which he acts that Chocka is impressed with. He also talks about the various inputs that Dhoni comes up with during shoots, at times leaving the now seasoned ad director with the feeling that 'he knows more about the field than I do'.

He can also put his clients on the spot. The same oil company once did a campaign with Dhoni called 'CEO of the Day' where Dhoni turned out in a dapper suit and was asked to go about his business like he was the main man. 'He fit into the role seamlessly. For me, that was another example of why he's a true leader. But what I didn't know was that, like with bikes, he can hold a conversation on anything. Like he really got the big officers of the company thinking with some of his questions. Like he asked, "With all these electrical cars and bikes coming into vogue, what happens to the oil your company keeps generating?" It was amazing,' Chocka recalls.

Dhoni's fascination with anything unconventional isn't restricted to guns and war. He's the same in the studio too. It's when Chocka and others of his ilk push him to be a part of their novel and inventive concepts that he gets most excited. Like the time he was asked not to be the hero for a change in an ad that involved a fan academy of Manchester United. Dhoni agreed to play the part of a Man U fan, which he is anyway, and despite having committed to only an hour, was very happy playing a minor role in the overall advertisement.

'Most of the others are very, very image-conscious. Dhoni is just plain practical even with ads. He never has any qualms with doing whatever is best for the product,' says Chocka.

The fourth season of the IPL was a seminal moment for the franchises in the league. There were two more added but it was the first time players were retained and club loyalties became an actual thing and not some foreseen gimmick. It also allowed those creating the ad campaigns around these teams to break the traditional mould and experiment a lot more. It meant Chocka could come into his own and, as a result, Dhoni warmed up to his director that much more.

Chocka takes pride in informing me that he was the first person to shoot the promotional images of Dhoni right after he'd shaved his head following the World Cup win in 2011. But before we get into that shoot, a little anecdote about the night Dhoni went bald.

The story goes that on the night of the World Cup final, once all the festivities had ended, Dhoni was in his room with his little entourage and a couple of teammates. While the conversation and jokes raged on, Dhoni disappeared into the bathroom. Some fifteen minutes later, there was a bit of concern around the room. There was no sign of Dhoni and even repeated knocks on the door were being ignored. But just as worry was about to turn into panic, they heard the door open. Sakshi was the first to spot him and is learnt to have screamed in surprise. For, there stood the man who'd won India the World Cup just a few hours earlier with the most famous six in Indian cricket history—and he had just gone bald.

Back in Chocka's studio, they had planned for something a little different with the CSK captain. Instead of the usual merchandise shots with the jersey, they wanted Dhoni in a more casual avatar, with his new hairdo and all.

By now, Chocka was taking liberties with Dhoni, and if anything, only making his trips to the studio a lot more satisfying. Often at the end of a shoot, his crew and staff would gather around Dhoni for the facile selfie, and most days, Dhoni would ask everyone to gather around and oblige them. Chocka though had a couple of unusual requests. First, he wanted Dhoni to pose for a picture for his personal collection where he was strangling the ad director. 'I told him, I take so much of your time and you're irritated with me, so just grab my neck. He was such a sport that he did it despite me telling him that it wasn't an official shoot.'

The next time, after what was an extensive shoot, Chocka went to him with another bizarre request. Now he wanted Dhoni to stand and pretend like he was throwing a punch and the director would jump back and be frozen mid-air, like in an action sequence in a Japanese movie.

'After seeing the reference shot, he said, "If you fly like that, you'll break your head." But I convinced him that I had practised it,' says Chocka. Dhoni did as he was asked to, and Chocka thought the shot was a super success. But Dhoni wasn't convinced. He didn't think he was shot at

the right angle compared to where I was for the shot to be
a success. Dhoni told Chocka that he would prefer it to be
perfect since it was for his personal collection and then, of all
things, he asked him whether he'd be okay doing it again.
'He was asking me whether I want to do it one more time.
I couldn't believe it. Here was M.S. Dhoni going out of his
way and taking interest in some personal photo I wanted.
That is M.S. Dhoni,' says Chocka, who did oblige Dhoni
and got the picture taken again, this time to perfection.

Back in 2006, a young Dhoni met with two officials from
a very popular dairy product company on the top floor at
Mumbai's Taj Gateway. The meeting had been set up by a
common friend in the hope that India's latest wicketkeeping,
ball-smashing sensation would have his first long-term
brand contract. The deal was pretty straightforward. It was a
retainer for Rs 6 lakh—those were simpler times when the
crore was still a mythical figure, catering only to a select few
in the higher echelons. There was also a suggestion to the
dairy company that they put in a right-to-reserve clause for
five to six years which would see a 10 per cent rise annually
in what Dhoni got. It was an endorsement deal made in
advertising heaven, if there is one. Here was the most
exciting new prospect in Indian cricket, with a reputation
for being a heavy milk consumer—allegedly drinking four
litres a day—signing up with one of the largest dairy brands
in the country. He had that *pehelwan* (wrestler) look to go
with it. But it wasn't to be.

'They said Rs 6 lakh is too much. What if he doesn't click?' the common friend recalls now with the same shock I assume he's carried for the last dozen years. A year later, Dhoni was named as India's captain for the World T20 tournament. He gave Joginder Sharma the last over in the final. Misbah-ul-Haq played that shot and Sreesanth took that catch. Then Dhoni's price tag, within twelve months, burgeoned to over a crore rupees. There was no turning back now. The deal that wasn't would forever remain a case of spilled milk. And anyway, nobody was talking about his milk consumption any more. It was all about fast bikes and a fast life. The desi pehelwan had landed on the big stage and was now on his way to become a global phenomenon.

The market was crowded. Sachin Tendulkar and Rahul Dravid still ruled the roost. Virender Sehwag wasn't far behind, leaving Dhoni in a head to head with Yuvraj Singh in the youth bracket. And Yuvraj had more going for him. He was glamorous, controversial and had the intrigue of the seductive kind. Dhoni, say those around him, wasn't prepared to make any overt changes to who he was. He was, they maintain, 'too comfortable and satisfied in his own skin'. So, he would target the youth-icon bracket in a subtler fashion.

'If you remember, he had given away his jersey to some young fan. And he lifted the World T20 trophy wearing a sleeveless jersey. Nobody else could have imagined doing it. That wasn't a coincidence. It was all worked out. He's too smart. He's not guarded but detests being a show-off. He doesn't like jargon. But this was perfect. It was a statement made without a sound,' says a close confidant. The Thala post now makes so much more sense.

The ad market, though, still remained too saturated. Dhoni eventually realized that till the time he made a proper breakthrough, it was prudent to adopt a '*jo mil raha hai, le lo*' (whatever you get, take it) approach.

'Tendulkar doesn't do jeans. I'll do jeans. Tendulkar does BMW, I'll do TVS. The hair worked perfectly,' says a friend.

Kakkar reveals that he was not in agreement with Dhoni over his early choice of ads, and his hairstyle. 'I would often say, "Yaar, it would be better if you started using conditioner on your hair; don't just wash it with Lifebuoy soap,"' he says with that characteristic guffaw, and adds, 'It was fancy to have long hair and all. But his hair was like straw. It wasn't soft, shiny or had any glow to get him a proper ad.'

For others though, he became a people's champion, a man whom you believed when he was selling you a ceiling fan, a pen or a detergent powder. He had that everyday-man authenticity about him. While most of his contemporaries were sticking to the global trend of endorsing higher-class products, be it cars, watches or even cola, Dhoni was breaking new barriers and reaching out to newer markets. And he was doing so without spreading it too thin.

'He could appeal to all classes and strata of society. He can become anything. He can look dapper in anything and connect with both a little child and a top-end executive, while also somehow looking the part in a

Tamil ad where he looks to be mouthing a very street-style dialogue like, *na vandhutenlaaa* (I've arrived, no),' says Chocka.

He has also been compared to India's greatest all-rounder, Kapil Dev, the man who cut ice with the top cream of the society and bridged them with the middle and lower classes. '*Palmolive da jawab nahi.* (There's no answer to Palmolive.) Even years later, if you asked anyone for Kapil Dev's most famous line, they'll still mention that one and not some cricketing quote. They first laughed at Kapil but had to stop laughing once he started performing. It's the same with Dhoni,' says Kakkar.

Kapil Dev too possessed a rustic charm that appealed to the masses. The 1980s, though, was a time when the fledgling ad industry in India was still obsessed with articulate, English-speaking and well-groomed cricketers. Kapil Dev was an anomaly who broke that trend,. Dhoni took it to the next level.

If Kapil was the game changer, industry experts believe Dhoni was the game breaker. It happened when Rhiti Sports entered the scene. 'I remember his earlier agents being greedy. They were all about *paise do, maal lo* (give the money and take your goods). It didn't matter what the product was or whether he fit the role. I used to be very critical of his ad choices then,' says Kakkar.

He's not the only one. Those around Dhoni from that period remember him being naïve, and he was being taken for a ride. This was one of the reasons he ended up handing over this part of his life to close friend Arun Pandey, who started Rhiti Sports.

'*Agar topi pehenane wala hi chahiye toh mere dost ko hi de deta hoon.* (If I am always going to be cheated, then let it be by a friend.) At least the money will go to my friend's house and not to some stranger,' he had joked once to his friend. Pandey has become an omnipresence around Dhoni ever since. There are those who say that it's an overbearing presence, but even they grudgingly admit to his efficiency in cutting the best endorsement deals for his friend and client.

'No lengthy meetings and stuff. He might not be the most articulate but he can get a deal done in minutes. And the best deals,' one says.

According to one sports management expert, someone who has the who's who of Indian cricket among his clientele, Dhoni and Rhiti Sports were responsible for the biggest boom that the cricket market had ever seen, till Virat Kohli came along. They did so by employing a master stroke: a press release in the year 2010 that said Dhoni was 'signed for Rs 210 crore by Rhiti Sports'.

'Minimum guarantees mean nothing. When a player grows, he starts getting chota (small) brands. It's a fine balance. At that point of time you have to decide whether you want to tie up with a guy for Rs 15 lakh or you want to wait for him to do well and the same 15 lakh will become 1 crore. After every duck your rate changes, and after every 100, your rate changes,' he explains.

At the time Dhoni signed up with Rhiti, Tendulkar was still demanding the highest amount of around Rs 2 crore in the Indian ad market. 'If I have a player whom I've signed for 210 crore, I'll tell the brand, "*Aapko kaise itna sasta mein de doon?* (How can I give you so cheap?) That becomes a great selling point. What Rhiti did, changed the contract scales from 1 to 2 crore to 9 to 10 crore per year. This ensured that even Sachin gained from it. So, the benchmark for the top two players became 6 to 10 crore,' he says.

The sports management guru explains that historically, Indian cricket has had two players sharing the spoils at any given time—Sachin and Azhar, Sachin and Jadeja, Sachin and Dravid, Sachin and Yuvraj, Dhoni and Yuvraj, and so on. And if you, as a management firm, didn't have one of the two top players, you were swimming against the tide. With Yuvraj's stock not in the same league any more, Dhoni was sharing the spoils at the top with Tendulkar.

In a way, when he signed up with Rhiti Sports, Dhoni was becoming his own manager. And deals started pouring in; behind each of them was Pandey finding the best price without fuss.

'That move also meant that Indian cricketers could now go head to head with the Bollywood bigwigs in the ad market. They had now entered the big league for good,' says the management guru.

And while Dhoni kept pushing the envelope both on and off the field, he also maintained goodwill by being loyal to those brands that had stuck by him when he was a nobody—that adage again of not to leave anyone stranded.

The ride, of course, hasn't always been smooth. Dhoni's silence over the spot-fixing scandal in 2013, increased scrutiny on his off-field associations. Then there was the conflict–of–interest allegations involving his stakes in Rhiti Sports, which also had other cricketers on board, and his position as Indian captain became an albatross around his neck. But Dhoni remained unstirred. He let Pandey do the talking, and the agent would go routinely on record about his star client not holding any shares in his company. Now it depends on which side of the fence you sit on with Dhoni—as an outsider, that is—to ascertain whether the issue ever quite got its closure or not.

On the other hand, Dhoni ended up leading India to that one global title that had eluded them, the Champions Trophy in 2013. It wasn't the first or only time an on-field feat had overshadowed, if not eclipsed, an off-field controversy surrounding a team or player. You just have to think back to Italy winning the FIFA World Cup in 2006 in the midst of one of the biggest fixing scandals in football history.

Perhaps Dhoni himself summed it up best on the eve of the World T20 final against Sri Lanka in 2014 when he said, 'There's hardly any good or bad in Indian cricket that happens without my name.'

Prahlad Kakkar is no stranger to getting superstar cricketers to shed their inhibitions and perform roles they wouldn't otherwise for the camera. He worked extensively with Sachin Tendulkar and so too with Rahul Dravid in later years. He puts Dravid and Dhoni in the same bracket in terms of their simplicity. Kakkar reveals how Dravid would often end up having lengthy chats in Marathi with his driver whenever he met him at the airport. He says Dhoni does the same.

But Kakkar finds a problem with the Dhoni voice. He says, 'His big problem, like with Sachin, is his voice. It isn't a baritone, and we would often have to enhance it to make it sound more authoritative.'

As for the Tendulkar comparison, Kakkar feels that unlike the star batsman, Dhoni took a while to become more conscious about the brands he was endorsing. This changed as he matured as a captain but friends say that he could never resist any ad which gave him a chance to ride a new bike.

Kakkar also feels that Dhoni has been underdone, unlike Tendulkar, by most of the ad directors who have not tapped into who he really is. To portray Dhoni as a flamboyant hero in almost every other ad is what he refers to as 'playing it safe'.

It's not like Dhoni isn't prepared to try something different. If anything, he thrives on it. He doesn't even mind being on the receiving end of a barb, like Chocka says. He even shares a video with me of an ad he's shot for a leading cement brand where the script is based around making fun of Dhoni. In it, he is seen trying his best to learn two lines in Tamil and seems ready when the director calls for action. He mouths off the two lines eloquently and looks very pleased with himself. The wide smile, however, vanishes when he hears a voice saying, 'Sorry, Dhoni, only stills today.'

'Dhoni's brand,' Kakkar tells me, 'is that of an outsider who gatecrashed the party. It is of an underdog who came from the wrong side of the tracks and won.' He then goes on to describe what his idea of a dream ad with Dhoni is, one where he would focus only on his strengths. 'His strength is introspection. His strength is doubt. His strength is his argument with himself. Am I good enough? Can I prove them all wrong? Portray Dhoni as who he is, a man with five million questions and doubts. And then he finally resolves himself saying, "To heck with it, I'm going to prove everybody wrong. I'm going to do it the only way I know." The Dhoni way.'

Perhaps the answer to our quest for discovering the real Dhoni lies in that must-be-made advertisement. For, his journey has been one based on self-education, and along the way, he has learnt that he's just Dhoni. A man who was not born to be a cricketer but became one. A man who was not born to be a captain but became one. A man who was not born to be a legend but became one. A man who was born to be an enigma and will always remain one.

10

The Man Emerges

'I'm Dhoni.' V.B. Chandrasekhar still sounds a tad staggered every time he recalls his first-ever encounter with Dhoni. More so when he narrates that last part where Dhoni knocked on his hotel room door at 10.30 in the night and introduced himself in the most matter-of-fact fashion possible. But to really fathom his astonishment, you'll need to know the background to this unique first meeting between the then national selector and the rookie wicketkeeper he'd never laid his eyes on before.

It was 29 March 2005, a day before the touring Pakistanis were scheduled to play a warm-up one-day match in Hyderabad. Chandrasekhar was on hand as the South Zone national selector doubling up as the manager of India A—a common practice back then—which had only one wicketkeeper in their squad. But by 7 p.m., there was no sign of Dhoni, and Chandrasekhar was getting concerned. 'I made a call to Pranab Roy, the East Zone selector then,

184

and asked him about this Dhoni's whereabouts. He simply said, "Don't worry, he'll come." I asked, "Where is he coming from?" But he just said, "No, no, he'll be there."'

Chandrasekhar, the former Tamil Nadu and India opener, hadn't even seen a picture of Dhoni at that point but had heard that he was an exceptional striker of the cricket ball.

Concern turned into near-panic by 9 p.m. as Dhoni remained absconding. An hour later, Chandrasekhar had more or less resigned to the fact that his team would go into the match the next morning without a specialist wicketkeeper.

'Hyderabad wasn't a big airport back then like now, and not many flights would land post 9 p.m. Plus, I knew he was coming from really far away,' he says. Then came the knock on his door, and an annoyed Chandrasekhar was just about to unleash himself on the long-haired, muscular man standing right outside.

'I wasn't used to seeing cricketers look like that. He looked very different with the hair and all and I was just about to throw him out when he told me who he was in just those two words. I just smiled back at him,' he recalls.

When he looks back now, it was Dhoni's overall disposition rather than the candour in his introduction that left a strong impression on Chandrasekhar. He had expected the young cricketer to not just take a few steps back when the door opened in a show of respect to hierarchy, but also look a little fidgety with his fingers not knowing where to keep them. 'None of that happened with MS though,' he says.

That first meeting was also when Chandrasekhar realized that M.S. Dhoni wasn't one for what he calls 'misplaced politeness'. But it did kind of set a funny precedent of sorts wherein the two would in later years—long after VB was done with his term as national selector and their three-year union at Chennai Super Kings—always jokingly introduce themselves to each other at every meeting. 'Hi, I'm V.B. Chandrasekhar.' 'Hi, I'm Dhoni.'

A few years after this first meeting, Chandrasekhar would receive another, more telling, reminder of that famed Dhoni self-confidence and his unflappable belief in who he was. It came during the first season of the IPL. Chandrasekhar was CSK director of operations and chief selector. Dhoni was the captain. CSK had made a successful start to their campaign, winning their first four matches before going down to Delhi Daredevils in an away match. Dhoni had won the toss and elected to bat despite having lost his two key top-order Australian batsmen, Matthew Hayden and Michael Hussey, who'd left for international duty. Chennai could only muster a middling total which the Daredevils chased down rather comfortably. Chandrasekhar had by now noticed a trend in Dhoni's decision-making at the toss which didn't sit well with him.

'I realized that Dhoni was just blindly deciding to bat after winning the toss. He was not weighing in the prevailing conditions, the opposition or their strength. He just felt that whatever the runs on the board, he could protect it like what he'd done in the World T20 final a year earlier. He seemed really sold on that idea and it was very difficult to wean him off it,' he says. So, Chandrasekhar tried impressing upon Dhoni that especially now with the Aussies gone and the bowling subsequently strengthened as a result with the entry of Makhaya Ntini and Muttiah Muralitharan, he should look to bowl first in helpful conditions.

Chennai's next match was against Rajasthan Royals in Jaipur where they were welcomed with a green-top. This was exactly the scenario in which Chandrasekhar had asked Dhoni to field first. Dhoni won the toss again, and he elected to bat again, much to the team director's chagrin. As it turned out, Pakistan's wrong-footed left-armer Sohail Tanvir cleaned up CSK with a magical 6/14, which still stands as the best bowling figures in the IPL. Chennai made only 109, which Rajasthan, after a stutter, chased down within fifteen overs. As the team made their way back, a livid Chandrasekhar made an announcement in the bus that the captain and coach would have to meet him as soon as they reached the hotel.

'That was year one, and I was behaving like I had been given a fabulous team and the team could do anything but lose. I suddenly found myself to be a taskmaster, not realizing that I was standing in front of some international greats. But it somehow didn't matter to me then,' he recalls.

Dhoni and Kepler Wessels, who was CSK's coach for that first season, showed up duly in front of Chandrasekhar, who let it rip and gave them both a piece of his mind, which he says 'wasn't very pleasant' and then walked away. Dhoni said nothing.

'Next day on the bus, I looked him in the eye and said, "Ah, I think I must have been a touch angrier than I should have." Dhoni looked at me and said, "You were very,

very, very, very angry . . ." and moved away. I couldn't
make anything out of that face. It was just a reminder that
he hadn't changed one bit from our first meeting,' says
Chandrasekhar.

Two things stood out for him that day, and they give us
another window into the myriad ways of the Dhoni mind.
He'd shown Chandrasekhar the respect he deserved as a
former cricketer and to his position as CSK team director
by politely brushing away the issue. But not without
reminding him of his temper.

'He didn't have to show that he was a subservient
kind of guy. Here's a World T20–winning captain and a
big name getting thumped by a team selector, that too in
front of the coach who's an outsider. But it didn't matter
to him. He was just there doing a job. He could have
turned his face around and said that wasn't the way to
behave or said so many things to me, but he was like,
okay, it happened, done and dusted, let's move on,' says
Chandrasekhar.

It's also perhaps a case of Dhoni never having been
one for a confrontation. He's not been one to indulge
in a mouthy exchange to get an upper-hand in a debate
either, not in the public space anyway. He's always fought
his battles at his own pace, in his own way, and with the
subtlety of a diplomat, even if it's not always been through
diplomacy but loaded wisecracks and puns. But it can often
be so obscure that probably even those it's intended for
don't get it. Or like he did with Chandrasekhar back in
2008, when he's put on the spot or criticized, he responds
with the same, strong message—silence.

There is a thin line between being strong-willed and being adamant. Dhoni has tiptoed and criss-crossed that line repeatedly as a captain. It could happen while backing a player or while doing his best to show up one that he didn't back. Rarely did he take off his pads and come on to bowl without it being a signal to the selectors about what he felt about the bowling arsenal at his disposal. Speaking of signals, Chandrasekhar recalls one that came his way back in 2008, soon after his outburst in the bus.

'I told him once you and I need to have a small chat after this game and he said, "Where do I have the time?" That was his defensive way of saying, "Let's not discuss things. Leave it. I am okay with doing what I am doing." That's when I realized that here is a guy who's going to be very adamant with what he wants to do . . . that's the reason why he would be successful in the years to come . . . because he had his own mind and he did not let other people mess around with it,' the former selector says. In 2016, when the World T20 tourney came to India, it was the International Cricket Council's (ICC) turn to find out that you simply can't force Dhoni's hand and make him do something he doesn't want to do.

The ICC and the broadcasters had come up with an idea before the event where they would get the captains of each team to read out their playing XIs into the microphone once the toss was done. As it turned out, India took on New Zealand at Nagpur in the opening game of the tournament. The first captain who would have to play the role of the makeshift announcer was Dhoni. But when the request was made to him, his answer was, as always, short and to the point. 'No, I don't think so,' he's learnt to have said. Just like that, the ICC's grand idea was dropped.

Dhoni had played all of three insignificant ODIs against Bangladesh at the time he made that dramatic late-night appearance outside Chandrasekhar's room. He didn't make much of an impression in the match that followed, scoring 3 off 9 balls on a bouncy Hyderabad pitch against a pacy Pakistan attack. But less than a week later, he was back in the then united state of Andhra Pradesh for what would prove to be a seminal moment not just in his life but in the history of Indian cricket. The 148 against Pakistan in Vizag on 5 April 2005 signalled the emergence of India's new cricketing superhero.

'I remember the Rajasekhara Reddy stadium in Vizag then was not finished and they had makeshift stands. The ball kept disappearing out of the ground very quickly, very often. Until then I had only seen Tendulkar's bat look as broad as a wooden bureau while connecting with the ball, especially when he hit shots past the bowler or extra cover. He had that Tendulkar thing about him,' Chandrasekhar says, recalling that stupendous knock against Pakistan.

Over the next two years, Chandrasekhar would play a crucial yet unsung role in shaping Dhoni's career, though he may have been unaware of it back then. His first contribution came during a selection meeting in Chennai later that year to pick the Test squad against Sri Lanka. Tamil Nadu's Dinesh Karthik had at that point cemented his spot as India's No. 1 wicketkeeper in the longer format since his debut exactly a year earlier. But he'd hardly done much with the bat in those ten Tests, averaging a mere 18.84 despite having been touted as a prodigious talent.

Not for the first time in his life and career, Dhoni had to fight the burden of the stereotype. He neither looked like nor, more importantly, seemed to have the game for Tests. He hadn't helped his cause with the breakneck speed at which he'd scored his 148 and 183 against Sri Lanka in the ODIs a few months earlier. The Karthik vs Dhoni debate was one that the More-led committee just couldn't make their mind up over.

'He'd already brought a massive change to India's batting in ODIs and I thought he could do the same in Tests. But I then said I leave it to the captain (Rahul Dravid) to decide. He said, "DK (Dinesh Karthik) has done really well but at this point of time somebody like a Dhoni would make a really big difference," and it all ended there. That was the first time I was involved in Dhoni's selection,' says Chandrasekhar.

That was only the first time. Two years later, he would play an instrumental role in redefining the geography of cricket fandom in the country. He would give Chennai their new Thala, and the city would never stop whistling again, even if he looked and sounded as alien to them as they did to him. The IPL storm was about to hit India. Cricket in the country would never be the same again.

Around a year after their first meeting, Chandrasekhar's term in the selection committee was over and he didn't come across Dhoni again till 2008. In that period, Dhoni had captained India to the first-ever World T20 title and emerged as the new poster boy of Indian cricket. India Cements, meanwhile, had become the owners of the Chennai franchise in the IPL. And Chandrasekhar was appointed in charge of all cricket operations.

The first month or so in his new role, he reveals, was spent sorting out the innumerable logistics involved with setting up a T20 franchise in India. He was also getting used to hearing about 'absurd amounts of money'. It's a good thing he was, for very soon he would be dealing with 'absurd amounts of money'.

The first-ever IPL players' auction took place on 20 February 2008 at a plush hotel in Mumbai. Chandrasekhar recalls having been handed a carte blanche by N. Srinivasan, the India Cements chief, to pick whoever he wanted, while the others on the auction table were clearly told to just sit and watch him raise the paddle.

But that free hand would be tested a few days before the auction, when the boss himself had a disagreement with Chandrasekhar's choice. 'I told him I wanted Dhoni. He was keener on Sehwag. I told him Dhoni was going to be the next biggest youth icon in the country and a big-ticket for our franchise, sounding as confident as I could. But he still kept saying Sehwag. By the next morning though, he had changed his mind—the first thing after waking up, he told me over the phone that he wanted Dhoni,' VB recalls.

Then the CSK management had to take a call on how much they would be willing to pay for Dhoni. On the eve of the auction, the predictive market rate for the most popular cricketer in the country was going up by USD 100,000 almost every fifteen minutes. When the team management meeting started on the eve of the auction, it stood at USD 1.3 million. But every time the team director worked out and adjusted the cut-off price accordingly, Rakesh Singh—now the company president and then the marketing president of CSK—would tell him it's gone up by another decimal point of a million. At USD 1.6 million, Chandrasekhar believed they had broken the bank only to be informed that the Dhoni stocks had risen by another 0.2 million.

'Rakesh told me with a wicked smile that "VB, it's 1.8 million now." I said, "Okay, let Mumbai have him. That way they'll have Dhoni at one end, Tendulkar at the other and be left with some 400 dollars to fill up the rest of their team." Honestly, it was only later that I realized that USD 1.5 million meant Rs 5 crore,' he says. Srinivasan, though, was by now adamant and the next morning, which was the auction day, he even made Chandrasekhar promise that he would give him Dhoni.

'He couldn't come for the auction before midday since he was performing his father's death anniversary ceremony in the hotel. But he said by the time he arrived, we should have Dhoni.'

Dhoni's base price was USD 400,000. The exchange rate on that day was Rs 39.84 to the dollar, and it tells you how cyclopean the growth has been both in terms of the money that the players, even the average ones, get bid for and, of course, about the dollar to rupee ratio. It didn't take too long for the bidding to reach the millions. At around the USD 1.2 million mark, all other teams dropped out of the race, leaving Chennai and Mumbai in a paddle-raising shootout. And it's here that Chandrasekhar decided to employ a 'playing possum' strategy to outfox his rivals.

'I was making the auctioneer call out twice before I raised the paddle and just as he was about to bang the hammer down. Every time Mumbai shot back, I would hesitate, look around like I am not going to do this, like this is too much and I am about to give up, and then raise it again,' he says. Around him, at his table, panic levels were going through the roof as they kept reminding Chandrasekhar that the boss wanted Dhoni at any cost. They were either not aware of or didn't agree with his tactics of not showing his hand or his team's desperation to get the man from Jharkhand.

When Mumbai took it up to USD 1.4 million, Chandrasekhar hesitated for so long that he recalls that the Ambani-led auction table almost began to celebrate, and that's when he pulled the trigger again and took the price up to 1.5 million. That was it. Mumbai backed out. Dhoni was a Super King. It's only fitting that Dhoni was bought by CSK with a very Dhoni-esque bidding strategy.

A few minutes later, just before the auctioneer called for a recess, Srinivasan entered the auction hall. Chandrasekhar recalls how he came straight to the CSK table and gave him a big hug. "He was super charged up and beaming like a child who'd got what he wanted. I had to tell him politely, "Sir, the auction is not over yet. We need to contain our joy a little," and he said, "Yes, yes, of course,"' VB says, laughing.

The auction came to an end and CSK finished with a reasonably strong squad. But Chandrasekhar and Srinivasan were now bracing for a barrage of questions from the media about why they had spent so much on one player.

'I just told him to say that it was because Dhoni is priceless. Exactly 30 seconds later, a camera was on him and a mike was stuck into his face. He flashed a smile and said just that. "He's priceless."'

A decade later, even 'priceless' sounds like an understatement for what Dhoni has brought to CSK. That's not to say that it has been a completely one-sided affair. Dhoni's brand appeal, as gargantuan as it is already, wouldn't have broken such barriers across the country if he hadn't made Chennai his cricketing home. No other celebrity, cricketing or otherwise, from the northern part of the country had ever made such a clean break and entered the Tamil psyche in Chennai, nor had they opened the door wide for anyone else like they did for him. The love and adoration for Sachin Tendulkar was universal and he has probably won more hearts in Chennai—one of his most successful grounds in the country—than anyone else in Indian cricket history. But somehow, even the Tendulkar brand has never quite breached the rather partisan local market in Tamil Nadu, like the Dhoni brand has. Dhoni has played his part too, buying the Chennai franchise of the Indian Super League (ISL) football for good measure to make himself even more of a Chennaiyan.

His proximity to Srinivasan—a major collateral of his association with CSK—though has always been a matter of great intrigue, speculation and, often, controversy. The 2013 IPL fixing scandal was only the tipping point. A year before that, Srinivasan, then in the capacity of BCCI president, was alleged to have personally saved Dhoni's captaincy reign after the then chief selector Mohinder

Amarnath reportedly wanted a change.* This came after India had suffered 4-0 drubbings in England and Australia. Srinivasan admitted to this recently in Rajdeep Sardesai's book *Democracy's XI* where he's quoted as saying, 'Yes it is true that I vetoed the decision to drop Dhoni as captain. How can you drop someone as captain within a year of his lifting the World Cup? What you call favouritism I say is my respect for a top-class cricketer's achievements.'

Chandrasekhar was with CSK for only the first three seasons of the IPL and gave up his role after the 2010 IPL which saw his team's maiden title win. And he recalls Srinivasan being very fond of Dhoni. 'There was something about Dhoni that he felt was almost like him, maybe in his younger days. It was something about him that N. Srinivasan really liked even back then,' he says.

Chandrasekhar says there's a similarity in the way both of them always thrived on being in the present and not worrying too much about what had taken place in the past. 'After that loss in Jaipur where I had lost my cool, I came back to Chennai still smarting. Srinivasan looked at me and said, "Why the long face, VB? Let me tell you something. These guys are paid professionals. They are paid to perform and that's what they will do. No point in you sitting like that,"' VB recalls.

Democracy's XI also has Dhoni on record about his relationship with Srinivasan, and the Gurunath Meiyappan issue. While denying having told the Mudgal committee—

---

* 'Dhoni Sacking Blocked by Board Chief: Amarnath', ESPNcricinfo, 11 December 2012, http://www.espncricinfo.com/india-v-england-2012/content/story/596796.html.

which had been appointed to probe the fixing scandal—that Srinivasan's son-in-law was a 'cricket enthusiast', he clarifies that he'd only said that Meiyappan 'had nothing to do with the team's on-field cricketing decisions'.

Some in the CSK set-up, who didn't want to be named, testify to this fact. For starters, they say that Dhoni, who has never been known to be much of a planner for T20 cricket, would not even hold team meetings. 'Dhoni doesn't do team meetings. Fleming used to do a bowlers' meeting at CSK. Dhoni used to say, "You guys have the meeting, let me know about the plan. Don't worry at all. If your plan fails, I have other plans." He never goes for team meetings,' says one of them.

According to one member of Dhoni's close circle, he makes it a point to announce the playing XI only once the team is inside the bus and there are no officials around. Incidentally, English seamer David Willey when asked during the 2018 IPL when he finds out whether he's playing or not would reveal, 'probably at 4 o'clock in the afternoon when MS wakes up'.

'I met him post that pre-tournament press conference in Mumbai at the 2013 Champions Trophy in Cardiff where India were playing their first match. He came after practice, smiled, and hugged me, and I said, "I'm really happy." He said, "Why?" I said, "*Teri hasi gayee nahi hai.* (Your smile has not vanished.)" The genuine smile is still there. He said, "*Dil saaf hai, hasne mein problem kya hai?* (The heart is clean, so why can't I smile?),"'recalls one of his closest friends in the media community.

Kiran More believes that while Dhoni never changed who he was; his entry into Indian cricket and his subsequent rise caused everyone around him to change the way they functioned. And most of it was for the good. It wasn't just in terms of what was happening on the field, but also on the periphery. At the ground level, Dhoni changed the way training sessions were held, and made it a more flexible process rather than just have the entire team turn up every time regardless of whether they were keen on it or not.

'It (the training session) used to be compulsory. It's not about taking anything lightly but working hard on areas where you need to work hard. Some people don't like to practise too much. Earlier, they would be forced to show up, but because Dhoni wasn't always someone who needed a long hit before a match, others too started making more out of practice sessions than just going through the motions,' says More.

He believes that while Dhoni was at the helm, even the BCCI had to change their act because of the invisible wall the captain always seemed to be surrounded by. Not only did he never allow the administration—despite his closeness with Srinivasan—to get the better of him; he never let them compromise on the free hand he sought as the leader of the team.

'He might have asked for gag orders on the players in terms of the media, which I believe was needed at that point, but he made sure his communication with the board was clear and there was no room for anyone to play games,' More explains. 'That's why I say he ended up changing the structure of Indian cricket.' That's probably why More believes that M.S. Dhoni's career should be turned into a case study.

Chandrasekhar recalls having had to change his approach to get through to the CSK captain, and by the third season, he felt he'd cracked the code. He'd realized that if you force an idea on Dhoni, he would just ignore both you and the idea. But if you as a coach or support staff would leave it open-ended, there was a chance he might at least consider using it.

So when in the 2010 season, Chandrasekhar found Sri Lanka's magician spinner Muralitharan to be struggling slightly with the ball, he decided to drop a suggestion to Dhoni, very gently.

'He was getting Ashwin to bowl four overs straight up and Murali would come in right after the strategic break by which time the batsmen would be ready to unwind and they were going after him. Dhoni agreed that Murali was short on confidence,' says Chandrasekhar. It was only natural, he adds, that the off-spinner's confidence was shattered, considering Dhoni would clobber him repeatedly in the nets during practice to the extent that Murali would come and tell the director with awe: 'The bugger is a monster.'

Chandrasekhar's view was that Ashwin could be stopped after three overs and Murali given his first over before the strategic break. Since the batsmen wouldn't generally risk losing a wicket—at least based on the trend back then—before the break, they might play Murali out and allow the legend to settle into his spell better.

'I said that and left it at that. Come the next game, believe it or not, he did just that. Now I couldn't go and tell him "thanks for listening". He would have definitely stopped doing it in the next match,' he quips. But it was a lesson for Chandrasekhar and subsequent coaches or team mentors on the best practices of presenting M.S. Dhoni with an idea—always as a passing suggestion rather than as a strong idea. It's no surprise then that the likes of Gary Kirsten and Stephen Fleming—and to an extent, even Duncan Fletcher—gelled so well with the Dhoni style of captaincy. They were all great cricketers in their own right but when it came to Dhoni, they preferred chipping in rather than weighing in when they had a suggestion to make.

Off the field, Chandrasekhar and Dhoni hit it off, but like most other relationships of Dhoni's, except within the handful in his circle, it was a case of not too far and not too close. At night the two would cross paths as Dhoni would be heading out for dinner and Chandrasekhar would be getting done with his *sandyavandanam* (evening prayers). 'I would have just smeared my forehead with ash and I would see him walking past with a Raina or someone else. I would say, "Why don't you take me along?" He would look at my forehead and say, "I don't want to spoil you,"' says Chandrasekhar. Another time, Dhoni ended up giving the team director a lesson on Indian history, his own version anyway. He told Chandrasekhar that his close friend—Arun Pandey—was a Pandit too, like the team director. So when he was asked what he was, Dhoni quipped, 'We are the ones who were ruling this country before you Pandits took over. I am a Rajput.'

Chandrasekhar also recalls the time Dhoni tried explaining to him about his love for bikes, and then midway realized he was getting nowhere and gave up. 'He said, "Do you know the feeling of riding at 225 miles an hour and the breeze hitting your chest?" And then he saw my clueless face and decided immediately that there was no point continuing.' When VB tried to further investigate by asking whether some bikes indeed had seven gears and if one of them was for reverse like in autorickshaws, Dhoni just politely smiled and walked away.

The two hardly met once VB parted ways with CSK before recently bumping into each other during a Tamil Nadu Premier League (TNPL) event. Chandrasekhar was there in his capacity as a team owner, the VB Veerans, and Dhoni was the chief guest. Once they were done with their jesting introductions to each other, Dhoni would tell VB, 'It's good to know you have a team. With you around, I know you'll pick the best team.'

In 2008, when Dhoni took over as CSK captain, he was still only into his fourth year of international cricket. And here he was thrust with the responsibility of leading some of the most celebrated cricketers of that era. With Matthew Hayden, Michael Hussey, Stephen Fleming, Muttiah Muralitharan, Makhaya Ntini and Jacob Oram, Chennai had an all-star lineup. Dhoni might have been the flavour of the season and been bought for Rs 5 crore, but the only team he'd captained at that point was limited-over teams, and for less than a year. So, how did those with much more international experience than the captain look up to him? This was also the first-ever IPL—and this was the first time foreign players were playing in such a league, and that too under a relatively unknown, homegrown captain.

'From the very beginning I could see these guys settling down under him. It wasn't a case of them not wanting to hurt Indian sentiments or anything. They genuinely believed they could win matches with him at the helm. They realized, and so did I, that M.S. Dhoni was a natural leader of men,' says Chandrasekhar.

Convinced he might have been, but Chandrasekhar couldn't quite get his head around how this young man who'd already broken new barriers in Indian cricket was leading a bunch of international superstars as if he'd been doing this all his life. So, he decided to ask the man himself. And the response he got from Dhoni, Chandrasekhar believes, sums up the man and the enigma.

'I don't show them that I'm the captain of the team,' were Dhoni's words.

Chandrasekhar then quickly shoots a query at me. 'Do you still want anything else to prove that he's different?' and bursts out laughing.

That Dhoni is different from any other cricketer to have come from India is a fact that keeps proving itself every day that he continues to remain active in international cricket. As someone who's dealt on a personal level with pretty much every cricketing megastar in the twenty-first century, Chandrasekhar has his own theory: 'When you meet a Tendulkar, you'll know he's a private person but also be hit by his unbelievable humility. A man more private than him was Dravid, polished and who built a career around his phenomenal temperament. Ganguly's grey cells were always working, not in a scheming way, but you knew he was always thinking. Laxman stood for simplicity while Sehwag defined an uncluttered mind. You could categorize all of them. But how do you put Dhoni in any one column? An enigma is someone whom you can't understand or comprehend or categorize. And he's remained unfathomable to me and everyone else.'

But Dhoni's biggest strength has been that despite being a paradox to the rest of the world, he's always known exactly who he is. Perhaps that's why he's never cared much about what the world has to say about him. And he doesn't need to knock on your door in the middle of the night to tell you that. For, he *is* Dhoni.

Those fellows at the Taj President lobby all those years ago did perhaps have a point. Dhoni has never looked like any other cricketer before or after him. He has never walked or talked or batted or kept wickets like anyone else before or after him. He's also ensured that Indian cricket will never be the same again, not after it has felt the Dhoni Touch.

Acknowledgements

This is a Dhoni book. So it had to be done Dhoni style. That meant I didn't step on the gas till the required run rate (or in this case the deadline) reached fever pitch. It also meant that the publishers of this book, my dear friend Radhika Marwah in particular, were left anxiously perched on the edge of their seats.

I mainly got the confidence to write the book once Sriram Veera—my colleague, mentor, and someone who I say with full authority considers me the brother he never wanted—put it across simply: 'Sundu, you anyway are used to writing full-page stories which are around 3000 words each. Think of this as writing fifteen of those.' In those couple of minutes, Sriram-bhai had rationalized the task at hand in a way only he can. There was no looking back from there.

The man responsible for my writing all those full-page stories, of course, is the only boss I've ever had—Sandeep

Dwivedi. Sandy Sir has had to deal with those 'close finishes' in terms of daily deadlines for the last decade. He believed in me being a cricket writer before I ever did. He kept throwing me into the deep end, and I can't thank him enough. I owe most of what I've achieved in this industry to his support, his trust and, of course, his patience.

My job was cut out from the beginning to somehow unravel a narrative far beyond what's out there. I bumped into an array of fascinating characters along the way, each of whom had been privy to the Dhoni enigma and his aura at different times in his life. I couldn't have done this without their help.

Chittu-bhai & Co. in Ranchi provided me a front-row seat as they relived some of their beloved friend's life events during my visit there, not to forget their unbelievable hospitality. Colonel Shankar Vembu was introduced to me as the person responsible for helping Dhoni pursue his vast military interests. But he perhaps provided some of the greatest insights ever into his fauji friend. I also thank Kiran More, V.B. Chandrasekhar, Prahlad Kakkar and Chocka for their valuable inputs.

Of course, to you, Mr Dhoni; I appreciate how you dealt patiently with my routine presence at almost every practice session you've been to over the last eighteen months across the world. Someday, I do hope to get the courage, like you did, to bid adieu to the long mane, or at least get those 'layers done' as recommended.

A Note on the Author

Bharat Sundaresan lives for West Indian cricket and pro wrestling, and is a raconteur of all things and metal music. He has covered cricket for the *Indian Express* for the last ten years—seven of which he spent tracking down the Jamaican cricketer, Patrick Patterson.

A Note on the Author